# TABLE OF CONTENTS

THIS PAGE INTENTIONALLY LEFT BLANK

# LIST OF ACRONYMS AND ABBREVIATIONS

| | |
|---|---|
| CCP | Chinese Communist Party |
| CMC | Central Military Commission |
| CPC | Communist Party of China |
| CPPCC | Chinese People's Political Consultative Conference |
| DPJ | Democratic Party of Japan |
| FBIS | Foreign Broadcast Information Service |
| FIFA | Federation Internationale de Football Association |
| GLF | Great Leap Forward |
| GPCR | Great Proletarian Cultural Revolution |
| IMTFE | International Military Tribunal for the Far East |
| KMT | Kuomintang |
| LDP | Liberal Democratic Party (of Japan) |
| LT | Long-Term (trade agreement) |
| MHW | Ministry of Health and Welfare |
| MOFA | Ministry of Foreign Affairs |
| PLA | People's Liberation Army |
| PRC | People's Republic of China |
| ROC | Republic of China |
| ROK | Republic of Korea |
| SCAP | Supreme Commander for the Allied Powers |
| SDF | Self-Defense Forces |

THIS PAGE INTENTIONALLY LEFT BLANK

# I.  INTRODUCTION

When assessing the complex historical relationships that China and South Korea have with Japan, a headline in the 21 August 1983 *People's Daily*, the Chinese Communist Party's (CCP) official newspaper, which read, "The Past, If not Forgotten, Is a Guide for the Future," reveals much about the Chinese perspective on history, but contrasts starkly with George Santayana's aphorism that "those who cannot remember the past are condemned to repeat it."[1]  In the context of lingering historical animosity against Japan, such disparity may reflect Chinese and, presumably, Korean desires for Japan to forget its wartime past by discontinuing honoring imperialistic memories. For the Chinese and Koreans, they remember the past all too well. As a consequence they violate their own dictum of forgetting the past in favor of keeping historical animosity against Japan alive to ensure Japan remembers its imperialistic past thus preventing a return to militarism—the Japanese charge that the Chinese and Koreans manufacture historical issues for political purposes. While the Chinese and Koreans wish to forget the past, Japanese provocative actions that harken back to unsettled historical grievances serve as a reminder that Japan has not forgotten its wartime past. Rather, certain Japanese provocative actions suggest that Tokyo adopts Santayana's perspective: remembering its militaristic past helps ensure its pacifist future.

One of the ways Japan antagonizes its neighbors is when the Japanese prime minister pays tribute to Japanese war dead through ceremonial worship at the Yasukuni Shrine in Tokyo—an event that Chinese and Koreans criticize as honoring Japanese imperialism. When Japanese prime ministers visit Yasukuni, they elicit responses from the People's Republic of China (PRC) and the Republic of Korea (ROK) that are widely known. What is less understood is what these responses can reveal about the starkly different political systems these two countries employ. The major research question this study explores is: How do different political systems in the People's Republic of China

---

[1] Nihon Keizai Shimbun in Japanese, September 8, 1983, in United States Foreign Broadcast Information Service, *Daily Report: Asia and Pacific* (Washington, DC: GPO) (hereafter referred to as FBIS *Asia*) September 15, 1983, 3; George Santayana, *The Life of Reason* (Amherst: Prometheus Books, 1998), 82.

and the Republic of Korea affect each central government's response to a historically significant event, in this case Japanese prime minister visits to Yasukuni? Additionally, how do their political systems affect the manner these responses are implemented? What impact, if any, does the political system have on governmental support or repression of anti-Japanese nationalism? This thesis seeks to address these questions.

Since 1951 (the year that Japan entered into a peace treaty with the Allied powers), Japanese prime ministers have visited the Yasukuni Shrine 64 times. Given the differences in the manner that democratic and authoritarian regimes respond to public opinion, observers may expect the two systems to respond differently to Yasukuni, but the study finds that they do not. The argument advanced in this thesis is that with respect to Yasukuni, the overwhelming majority (90 percent) of responses from Beijing and Seoul were similar (in that both either ignored the visits or protested them), thus demonstrating that the difference in political system had little impact on the approaches both governments took to these visits. Economic status, rather, played a greater role in governmental response to Yasukuni. While political systems may not have shaped the responses, they were important in the way each government responded to public opinion. Lastly, when either government objected to official visits to Yasukuni, the evidence reveals that the underlying motivation for both governments was and remains the same: To prevent a resurgence of Japanese militarism.

## A.    IMPORTANCE

Japan is plagued by the memory of 20th century atrocities it committed in China and Korea. In the decades since World War II, Japan emerged as a global economic power relative to the PRC and the ROK. During Japan's rise, the Japanese government attempted to atone for its wartime past by apologizing for its imperialism and by normalizing relationships with its neighbors, the ROK in 1965 and the PRC in 1978.[2] Despite Japan's successful establishment of diplomatic relations with both countries and

---

[2] Japan's first recorded postwar apology was in 1965 by Japanese Foreign Minister Shiina Etsusabruo at the conclusion of the normalization treaty in Seoul. According to Wakamiya Yoshibumi, Shiina stated, "We feel great regret and deep remorse over the unhappy phase in the long history of relations between the two countries." Quote from Wakamiya Yoshibumi, "'The Law of Next Year' in Japan's Politics" *The Asia-Pacific Journal: Japan Focus* (2006), last accessed March 4, 2013, www.japanfocus.org.

its postwar economic success, neither country has forgotten nor forgiven Japan for its imperialist past. This historical animosity often provokes anger in the news and discolors bilateral relationships between Japan and its neighbors. One event that serves as a highly controversial link between past and present is Japanese prime minister visits to the Yasukuni Shrine. The conventional wisdom on Yasukuni posits that up to 1985, Japanese prime ministers visited the shrine without incident.[3] Since then, Japanese officials' visits to Yasukuni have become highly politicized and are perceived as a symbol of an unrepentant Japan honoring its militaristic past. Yet what is overlooked in the nationalistic reactions these visits trigger in the PRC and the ROK is that the two countries have completely different political systems.

The current perspective on Chinese and South Korean government responses to Japanese provocations suggests that these governments support popular anti-Japanese movements when it suits their interests and repress them for the same reason. What is needed is a comparison between each government's response to a significant Japanese action that has historically proven controversial in generating popular anti-Japanese nationalism among both audiences. Japanese prime minister visits to the Yasukuni Shrine since 14 class-A war criminals were interred there in 1978 have typically provoked such nationalistic emotions, and therefore they serve as an appropriate occasion to observe Chinese and South Korean governmental responses. Chinese and Koreans consistently protest official visits to the shrine, affording the opportunity to assess each government's response to each visit.

Moreover, it is appropriate to assess the prevailing status of bilateral relations of China and South Korea with Japan. If these governments act in a similar fashion—supporting or repressing anti-Japanese movements according to their needs—then the revelation that an authoritarian and a democratic regime respond similarly to the same provocation would contribute significantly to the understanding of Chinese and South

---

[3] Evidence proves that China objected to state sponsorship of Yasukuni as early as 1969, and the People's Daily lodged its first official criticism of the Japanese prime minister in 1983, thus discrediting the claim that Yasukuni became an international flashpoint in 1985. See Peking NCNA in English, April 16, 1974, in FBIS Asia, April 17, 1974, A14; Nihon Keizai Shimbun in Japanese, September 8, 1983, in FBIS *Asia*, September 15, 1983, 3.

Korean bilateral relations with Japan. Such analysis may also reveal when each government is more likely to respond in a negative way to Yasukuni Shrine visits, which may aid in assessing Tokyo's calibration of national policy on official visits to the shrine.

While this thesis addresses visits to the Yasukuni Shrine as the focus of its analysis, the importance of its findings may have far-reaching potential beyond the shrine. The real inquiry is not about reaction to visits to the Yasukuni Shrine per se, but rather on the response the visits elicit in an authoritarian regime versus a democratic one. Findings that reveal similarities or differences in the types of governmental responses or the frequency thereof could be applied to other areas of historical friction between Japan and its northeast Asian neighbors: the Nanjing atrocity, the comfort women, Japanese history textbooks, etc.

Unresolved historical grievances seem to be a major contributor to the suboptimal relationships between Japan and its neighbors. Improving the situation—not just between the three countries involved but in the entire region—requires all involved to get past history. A small but important step towards that goal is figuring out how, when, and why historical issues are kept alive.

## B.    THE LITERATURE

The existing literature on Chinese and South Korean government response to Japanese prime minister visits to the Yasukuni Shrine focuses mostly on the Chinese response from 1985 onward and, to a much lesser degree, the South Korean response from 2001 onward. Very little attention has focused on South Korean government reactions to shrine visits, and the little that has done so is thin regarding how, when, and why the ROK government responds to the Yasukuni visits. None of the literature surveyed in this review compares intergovernmental responses to Japanese prime minister visits to the shrine in China and South Korea.

The following review focuses on what academic and policy authors have to say about Chinese and Korea anti-Japanese nationalism vis-à-vis Yasukuni. The survey focuses on China, then South Korea, and lastly Japan.

## 1. China

In *China Eyes Japan*, Allen Whiting argues that perceptions and misperceptions of Japanese foreign and domestic policy are the cause of Sino-Japanese tension. He concludes that political issues outweigh economic cooperation between the two and that the prospect for improved bilateral relations depends largely on the signals that Tokyo sends to Beijing. Among the political problems that divide the two countries, the Yasukuni Shrine visits stand at the forefront. Whiting argues that visits by any Japanese official are likely to arouse anti-Japanese sentiment among the Chinese. He highlights Japanese Prime Minister Nakasone Yasuhiro's official visit to the Yasukuni Shrine in August 1985 as *the* event that occasioned mass anti-Japanese student protests in Beijing. These protests threatened to undermine Beijing's hopes for Japanese assistance in Chinese economic modernization initiatives, namely through CCP General Secretary Hu Yaobang's formation of a Commission for Sino-Japanese Friendship in the Twenty-first Century.

Whiting notes that Japanese Prime Minister Suzuki Zenko's Yasukuni visit in 1982 did not inspire national outrage because it was not made in an official capacity. However, such a conclusion presumes that everyone can and will distinguish an official visit from an unofficial visit each time. Can a head of state ever separate himself from his status? Moreover, multiple media sources in Beijing and Tokyo indicate that Suzuki's visit was in fact done in an official capacity, thus calling Whiting's assertion into question.[4] Whiting's work was published in 1989, so further analysis of shrine visits beyond 1987 are required to test his assumptions.

What Whiting's research lacks is an adequate analysis of why Beijing repressed popular protests in 1985. He makes a clear distinction between the response from Chinese society and the regime: politically charged events such as visits to the Yasukuni Shrine will continue to aggravate Sino-Japanese relations at the mass level regardless of whether the regime protests it or not. If Whiting's assertion is true, then with regard to the regime's role in leading or following public opinion, three possibilities emerge: (1) the

---

[4] See "Japan Holds Memorial Service" in Xinhua, (15 August 1982) and Asahi Shimbun (16 August 1982) article.

protests are popular and not supported by Beijing, and so suppressed; (2) popular protests are provoked or stimulated by Beijing; or (3) the protests are popular in origin but are supported or manipulated by Beijing. Based on Whiting's evidence, the relationship between leading and following is not clear.[5]

Lastly, one could build upon Whiting's work by analyzing the impact of a country's political system in response to perceived manifestations of rising Japanese nationalism, such as visits to the Yasukuni Shrine. According to Whiting, "The basic obstacle to better Sino-Japanese relations lies in the gap between an authoritarian system that grants party and government a directing role over all public aspects of society and a pluralistic, democratic system in which public diversity within both government and society is necessary and proper."[6] What happens when Whiting's assertion is applied to a democratic country instead of an authoritarian one? If the ROK, which has had a democratic government since the late 1980s, responds in a fashion similar to its authoritarian counterpart, what does that reveal about Whiting's conclusion that the key factor towards resolving historical animosities in Northeast Asia is the political system?

In *China's New Nationalism*, Peter Gries argues that Beijing has demonstrated that it will either support or repress anti-Japanese social movements depending on its interests at the time, particularly with regard to matters of international prestige. A key issue Gries addresses regarding anti-Japanese social movements is the difference in East and West understandings of Chinese nationalism: Chinese analysts view Chinese nationalism as a bottom-up movement, whereas Western analysts view it as a top-down propaganda tool of the CCP; though it could also be a combination of both.[7] Gries's dichotomy of interpretation moves beyond Whiting's analysis and submits that Chinese society will view provocative Japanese actions as antagonistic and revisionist at heart, and the people will respond regardless of whether the Party responds or not.

---

[5] Allen Whiting, *China Eyes Japan* (Berkeley: University of California Press, 1989), 197.

[6] Ibid., 185.

[7] Peter Gries, *China's New Nationalism: Pride, Politics, and Diplomacy* (Los Angeles: University of California Press, 2004), 119.

6

Gries's work is helpful in understanding the Chinese approach to Chinese nationalism. But his work does not discuss controversy in China over official visits to the Yasukuni Shrine. How Beijing has reacted to Japanese prime minister visits and the implications of its reaction may reveal regime intentions.

In *China: Fragile Superpower*, Susan Shirk argues that China is a "brittle, authoritarian regime that fears its own citizens and can only bend so far to accommodate the demands of foreign governments."[8] She contends that the regime's worst fear is a "national protest movement of discontented groups . . . united against the regime by the shared fervor of nationalism.[9] If Shirk is correct, then her argument supports the theoretical point of departure that Chinese nationalism is a bottom-up movement to which the CCP responds.

Shirk discusses some of the actions that the regime took in with respect to anti-Japanese protests in 2005. The People's Police and the People's Armed Police supported student protests in 2005 in Beijing, but only up to a point. They prevented the violence from escalating to an unmanageable level. Further illustrative of the regime's management of protests, the CCP Propaganda Department imposed a media blackout leading up to the protests. These crowd and information control measures illustrate some of the techniques the regime uses to allow its citizens to direct their anger outward, rather than inward, without losing control of the situation.

Regarding interests that drive the CCP to tolerate such protests, Shirk highlights Yinan He's observation that China learned a lesson from South Korean democratization. According to Shirk, "In South Korea during the 1960s, public protests against what people viewed as the weak stance of the country's dictatorial leaders in dealing with Japan fueled the movement toward democracy—the same thing could happen in China."[10] Not only does Shirk's assertion reveal why Beijing might tolerate nationalist

---

[8] Susan Shirk, *China: Fragile Superpower* (New York: Oxford University Press, 2008), 5.

[9] Ibid., 7.

[10] Ibid., 145.

social movements, it also provides some insight into the ROK government's experience of satisfying nationalistic demands in the 1960s.

Lastly, Shirk describes that the extent of Chinese frustrations with the Japanese government extended beyond prime minister visits to the shrine. A 2005 speech by PRC Ambassador to Tokyo Wang Yi stated that Beijing desired not only that the Japanese prime minister stop visiting the shrine, but also his top administration officials—the chief cabinet secretary and the foreign minister.[11] Wang's recitation of Chinese demands may be transferable to Koreans'.

In *Strong Society, Smart State: The Rise of Public Opinion in China's Japan Policy*, James Reilly contends that, contrary to Susan Shirk's thesis, China is not a fragile state fearful of its own society. It is rather a flexible regime that implements a strategy of "tolerance, responsiveness, persuasion, and repression" in response to "the rise of public opinion in Chinese foreign policy."[12] Central to Reilly's argument is that Chinese public opinion matters. According to Reilly, Chinese public opinion by the early 2000s was largely distrustful of and hostile towards Japan, creating limits on Beijing's Japan policy. Reilly's argument rests largely on two pillars: (1) political opportunities; and (2) Chinese control over the media.

Reilly uses Prime Minister Koizumi's visits to the Yasukuni Shrine in 2001 and 2002 to illustrate how political fragmentation creates opportunities for public mobilization.[13] He cites the transition from Jiang Zemin to Hu Jintao in 2002–03 as an instance of state-society interaction during which party leaders sought to improve Japan relations at the peak of a Yasukuni flare up. In this context, Beijing's Japan policy played out in a context of divisions among political elite and tensions in bilateral relations, which together provided opportunity and incentive for public opinion to influence foreign policy.[14]

---

[11] Ibid., 163.

[12] James Reilly, *Strong Society, Smart State: The Rise of Public Opinion in China's Japan Policy* (New York: Columbia University Press, 2012), 220.

[13] See Sidney Tarrow, *Power in Movement: Social Movements and Contentious Politics* (Cambridge: Cambridge University Press, 2011).

[14] Reilly, *Strong Society, Smart State*, 214.

Reilly's argument that Beijing possesses a capacity to respond flexibly and to adapt quickly to public opinion rests largely on its ability to control the media. If the regime controls the information that the public receives, then it can persuade society to move in the direction it desires. Through this mechanism the regime can manipulate anti-Japanese protests, knowing that it can turn the nationalistic tide in the opposite direction when needed. Reilly's theory comports with Whiting's notion that authoritarian regimes enjoy control over society, which is a fundamental difference from a democratic regime. It also matches Shirk's assertion that "the CCP will do whatever it takes to make sure that the information reaching the public through the commercial media and the Internet does not inspire people to challenge party rule."[15]

## 2.      The Republic of Korea

How then does a democratic nation like South Korea manage public opinion about Japan and its provocative actions?  In his article, "South Korea in 2001: Frustration and Continuing Uncertainty," Ha Chool-yong assesses the state of Korean-Japan relations in 2001, just before Koizumi announced a visit to the Yasukuni Shrine. He describes the Korean media backlash against Koizumi, but the details he offers are limited. More importantly, Ha's article links the shrine to another historical friction point: textbooks. In this context one might conclude that the Koreans only voiced discontent with the shrine out of the opportunity to pile on to the issue of the Japanese whitewashing history in school textbooks.

Moon Chung-in and Suh Seung-won argue that a Northeast Asia security dilemma is caused by "national identity and the politics of nationalism, which are closely intertwined with collective memory of history."[16]  With regard to the ROK, Moon and Suh claim that assertive nationalist sentiments cause Koreans to be suspicious and distrustful of Japan in a way that economic interdependence cannot ameliorate. Prime

---

[15] Susan Shirk, "Changing Media, Changing China," in *Changing Media, Changing China*, ed. Susan Shirk (New York: Oxford University Press, 2011), 3.

[16] Chung-in Moon and Seung-Won Suh, "Identity Politics, Nationalism, and the Future of Northeast Asian Order," in *The United States and Northeast Asia*, eds. G. John Ikenberry and Chung-in Moon (Lanham: Rowman & Littlefield, 2008), 194.

Minister Koizumi's visits to the Yasukuni Shrine stand as only one of several Japanese provocations offending Korean nationalism that impedes Seoul-Tokyo ties, despite relationship-building initiatives such as the 1998 Joint Declaration on Future Partnership and the 2002 joint hosting of the World Cup. While most would agree that Koizumi's visits did damage bilateral relations, Moon and Suh do not analyze why Korean nationalism was piqued in 2001, but not at any other time. The implication is either that previous Japanese prime minister visits did not provoke Korean nationalism, or that it did but not to a degree worth mentioning. Either way there is a gap in the information. Moon and Suh present plausible reasons why the ROK government did not propagate anti-Japanese sentiment in the late 1990s; however, such an inference merits further investigation.

Moon and Suh provide interesting statistical analysis of Korean and Chinese perceptions of Japan. Based on the results of a regional cooperation survey, they found that 90 percent of South Korean respondents and 87 percent of Chinese respondents viewed history as "a major impediment to regionalism" and that among those the majority of South Koreans believed historical issues were insoluble.[17] While these data are useful in establishing a potential baseline of where South Koreans or Chinese stand on historical issues with Japan, they seem inconsistent with past behavior. If history is so important to these audiences, then why were previous Japanese prime minister visits to the Yasukuni Shrine ignored?

Moon and Suh discuss the differences between the Kim Dae-jung administration and that of Roh Moo-hyun. Kim seemed more inclined to strengthen bilateral relations with Japan whereas Roh took a more adversarial position. Interestingly, Japanese prime ministers visited Yasukuni under both administrations, so what explains the divergent outcomes? One hypothesis is that the media of 2002 may have been more robust in terms of speed of reporting and enjoyed wider audiences than in 1998, which might explain why media sensationalizing of Yasukuni was greater in 2002 as compared to 1998. Another approach may be to focus on any major domestic policy initiatives over time and

---

[17] Ibid., 213.

10

their economic precedence over historical animosity. For example, did the East Asian Financial Crisis of 1997–98 play any role in Kim Dae-jung's calculus on whether to work with Japan for much needed economic support versus fighting with Japan over Yasukuni?

In *Japan and Korea: The Political Dimension*, Lee Chong-sik provides an in-depth analysis of the political interactions between the governments of Japan and South Korea from 1960 to 1985. He explores many of the highs and lows in the bilateral relationship, the domestic and international factors that influenced it, and the overall direction that each government sought to pursue vis-à-vis the other. Lee's work provides perspectives that one can use to link Japanese and Korean policy initiatives together with known dates of Japanese prime minister visits to the shrine to infer what might have been the motivation or rationale on the part of the ROK government to ignore visits to the shrine.

### 3.　　Japan

Richard Samuels, a prominent American specialist on Japan, offers a helpful account of the Yasukuni Shrine from the Japanese perspective. According to Samuels, "Virtually every postwar prime minister, regardless of political orientation, visited Yasukuni while in office, including the mainstream Yoshida Shigeru (ten times) and the anti-mainstream Nakasone Yasuhiro (eleven times)."[18]　He notes that in 1978 priests secretly interred 14 Class A war criminals, making Yasukuni a "lightening rod for historical memory."[19]　His data show that the majority of Chinese (60 percent) view the shrine as a symbol of militarism. Samuels claims that Yasukuni serves as a "barometer of one's view of the colonial experiences of China and Korea and, by implication, of history and politics more generally."[20]

Samuels highlights the significance of Japanese Prime Minister Nakasone's 15 August 1985 visit to the shrine as historically significant because it was the first visit of a prime minister after the shrine's politicization resulting from the enshrined war criminals.

---

[18] Richard Samuels, *Securing Japan* (Ithaca: Cornell University Press, 2008), 114.

[19] Ibid.

[20] Ibid.

11

However, Prime Ministers Fukuda Takeo, Ohira Masayoshi, and Suzuki Zenko each visited Yasukuni after the 17 October 1978 interment of the Class A war criminals, which lessens the validity of the popular argument that Nakasone's 15 August 1985 visit was of the magnitude for which it is now credited. Such an inconsistency in the data may reflect the relatively low key Chinese response observed in 1982 and 1983 as compared to 1985, but further begs the question of why the governments in China and South Korea chose to make an issue of one but ignore the others. Upon answering that question, one could take the inquiry one step further and analyze what specific actions the governments implemented in 1985 that they did not implement in earlier years. Answering both of these questions would greatly contribute to the existing body of knowledge on when, why, and how these governments elect to promote animosity towards Japan. Samuels goes on to say, "They [Japan's new mainstream conservatives] point out that between 1978, when the fourteen Class A war criminals were enshrined, and 1984, Japanese prime ministers visited Yasukuni twenty times without any objection from Beijing. This, they insist, is evidence that Beijing has manufactured the Yasukuni problem for its own political purposes."[21]

Claiming that Beijing uses anti-Japanese sentiment—whether aroused by Yasukuni Shrine visits, textbook revisions, or offensive public statements diminishing Japanese culpability at Nanjing—is in keeping with Greis's thesis that Beijing supports and represses anti-Japanese social movements as it suits its interests, particularly in gaining and maintaining face. What is missing from this theory is analysis of the domestic and international context in which the regime supports or represses these movements, and the Korean angle is almost completely ignored in these works.

Shibuichi Daiki argues that of all the visits to the Yasukuni Shrine, Prime Minister Nakasone Yasuhiro's in 1985 and Koizumi Junichiro's in 2001 were the most significant in terms of triggering animosity in China and South Korea because these visits were official in the sense that the visit was announced as such or the Japanese government paid the entrance fee to the shrine. According to Shibuichi, prior to 1985

---

[21] Ibid., 125.

visiting the shrine was normal and did not cause international outrage, which begs the question of what happened in 1985 that politicized the issue? Shibuichi merely identifies Nakasone's visit as sparking the flames of international controversy with China, but he does not explore the issue of why the Chinese took such issue with the visit (Shibuichi even points out that the Chinese largely ignored the 1979, 1980, and 1981 visits). The 1985 visit was met with harsh criticism by Beijing, which was then followed by mass Chinese protests months later. This is an interesting angle on China's side of the argument. Whiting and Gries would argue that the norm is for Chinese citizens to take issue with shrine visits and that the regime responded to public opinion according to its interests. Yet here we see the regime taking the lead and the people following.

Shibuichi attempted to analyze the South Korean reaction to the shrine visits as well. His argument is that the Korean reactions are similar to how the Chinese "see the shrine as honoring Japanese militarism and by extension the Nanjing massacre," Yasukuni honors the oppressive Japanese rule to Koreans, and therefore merits outrage.[22] According to Shibuichi, "The Seoul government applies pressure in much the same way that China does, except that Korea does not have a party- or state-owned media through which to express official opinions. However, the Korean mass media have excoriated Japan and many public demonstrations against Japan have been staged."[23] Shibuichi notes that Seoul only registered its objection to Yasukuni during Koizumi's visits starting in 2001. Shibuichi admits, "Why Korea waited until 2001 to join China in opposing and protesting a Japanese prime minister's visit to the Yasukuni Shrine is an intriguing question but outside the scope of this article."[24] Clearly the Korean angle on this issue has been largely ignored and merits research and analysis.

## C.    METHODOLOGY AND SOURCES

To discover why the preponderance of PRC and ROK responses to Japanese prime minister visits to Yasukuni were similar, a historical study and comparative

---

[22] Daiki Shibuichi, "The Yasukuni Shrine Dispute and the Politics of Identity in Japan: Why All the Fuss?" *Asian Survey* 45, no. 2 (2005): 213.

[23] Ibid., 205.

[24] Ibid., 211.

methodology of Chinese and South Korean governmental reactions was used. Information was gathered on the shrine and all prime minister visits since the signing of the San Francisco Peace Treaty in 1951. Once the data set was built, source documents were researched to gauge the response from both the PRC and the ROK.[25]  In cases where no observable response could be proven, a non-response was attributed to that government, implying that the event was either ignored or did not hold enough significance to take any observable action. In these cases where visits were ignored, research was conducted to determine the state of Chinese and South Korean bilateral relations with Japan to assess if any economic or other initiatives could help explain why these governments would ignore what each viewed as a provocative event.

Observed PRC and ROK governmental responses fell into two primary categories— similar and different—with a secondary subset of either ignoring the visit or lodging official protest. A "similar" response indicates that both governments either ignored or protested the visit; conversely, while a "different" response would normally indicate that one government protested while the other ignored, the evidence suggests that there was never an instance that the ROK protested but the PRC ignored. Thus, a different response indicates that the PRC protested while the ROK ignored a given visit. Noting when these two governments behaved similarly or differently is an important conclusion for its own sake, but an equally helpful finding is not just the consistency of the response but knowing when each government ignored or protested visits. A combination of the findings of consistency of response and also type of response hold the potential to advance understanding of when and why these governments are most likely to raise objections over this recurring event of historical symbolism.

---

[25] Primary source documents, including official press statements, communiqués, and government documents, were used to establish each government's position on visits to the shrine, or in relation to Japan more broadly. Secondary sources—including scholarly books on Chinese and Korean nationalism, academic or regional journals, and news media—were used to gather information on visits to the shrine and the reactions to them. The thesis used the Foreign Broadcast Information Service's *Daily Report* series (up to 1996) and the Open Source Center database (1996 to present) in an effort to include translated Chinese, Korean, and Japanese primary source documents, press reports, and opinion pieces. Each of these measures was considered across time to establish consistencies or differences between political parties in all three countries.

Once the information on the visits was gathered, the thesis assessed the general reaction to each in the PRC and ROK. How did the governments respond? How did society in general respond? If the response differed between government and society, what might account for that difference? What was the status of bilateral relations between the PRC and ROK with Japan? What policy initiatives were being pursued that might influence government support or repression of public protests? Were these initiatives agreed to by all, or were there dissenters in the government; if so, did the opposition promote a different public response than what was endorsed by the majority? Lastly, what similarities and/or differences exist in the way China responded to the visits and how South Korea did? What trends or patterns emerge?

Lastly, a note on naming convention: throughout this thesis all efforts were made to transcribe Japanese names with the surname listed first, which is common practice in East Asia.

## D.    THESIS OVERVIEW

The study begins by putting the Yasukuni controversy in its historical context. A brief introduction to the Yasukuni Shrine and the Japanese prime ministers who have visited while serving in that capacity since 1951 provides readers with an appreciation of why the Chinese and Koreans take issue with a Japanese cemetery (those unfamiliar with the Shinto faith may not draw a distinction between a cemetery and a shrine). Moreover, understanding the politicization of the shrine is crucial to understanding Chinese and Korean nationalism the controversy evokes today.

Next, the thesis defines political systems and state leadership in the PRC and in the ROK. The PRC, an authoritarian regime since its founding, enjoys certain freedom of action uncommon in representative governments. The Korean case is useful as the Republic began authoritarian, but then democratized in the late 1980s. The leadership of each government is discussed as it has direct consequence on the observable behavior with regard to Japanese provocations.

The thesis then moves into the historical study of Japanese prime minister visits to the shrine. The analysis begins with China and then moves to South Korea. Each country study attempted to examine sufficiently the aforementioned questions before moving on. Each country's historical study concludes with the author's observations as to how the central government responded to each visit in comparison to its policy initiatives, both domestic and international.

Following the historical study, the thesis compared the two countries, China and South Korea, and discusses the similarities and differences that were observed, and what these findings reveal about the significance a country's political system has on nationalism in relation to an event of historical significance.

The study closes with the author's conclusions on Chinese and South Korean bilateral relationships with Japan vis-à-vis the Yasukuni Shrine and policy implications for Tokyo.

## II. SHINTO AND YASUKUNI

### A. SHINTO

To understand Yasukuni and the controversy surrounding it, one needs a basic understanding of the Shinto faith. Shinto is the indigenous religion of the Japanese. According to Dr. Sokyo Ono, while the religion is one of the oldest in the world, the earliest record of the word "Shinto" was found in the *Nihon Shoki* ("Chronicles of Japan"), compiled in the early eighth century.[26] Ono emphasizes how Shinto is more than just a religion—it is a way of life: "It is an amalgam of attitudes, ideas, and ways of doing things that through two milleniums [sic] and more have become an integral part of the *way* of the Japanese people."[27]

Shinto is uniquely different from Western religions. First and foremost, Shinto has no central religious figure or religious text, making it unique amongst many organized religions, but difficult for non-Japanese to understand. The core of the Shinto faith is the worship of "*kami*," which can best be translated into "spirit." The Japanese who worship *kami* typically do so at Shinto shrines, either privately in their homes or publicly at local or national shrines. Unlike Western religions, Shinto worship is not conducted in mass gatherings, but rather individually and consists of four simple elements: purification, offerings, prayer, and a symbolic feast. Honoring one's ancestry makes Shintoism intensely personal and reflects the distinctive Japanese culture of worshiping *kami* through deliberate acts of religious ritual.

What exactly are *kami*? According to Dr. Ono, among *kami* are "the qualities of growth, fertility, and production; natural phenomena, such as wind and thunder; natural objects, such as the sun, mountains, rivers, trees and rocks; some animals; and ancestral spirits."[28] It is the last category that is of particular importance to this study: the spirits of national heroes and those who gave their lives in service defending Japan.

---

26 Ono Sokyo, *Shinto: The Kami Way* (Rutland: Tuttle Publishing, 1962), 2.

27 Ibid., 3.

28 Ibid., 7.

## B.    YASUKUNI

### 1.    History of the Shrine

Prior to the Meiji Restoration in 1868, the Tokugawa Shogunate essentially ruled Japan.[29] The Tokugawa Shogunate (1603–1868) successfully ended the warring states period (*sengoku* era, 1467–1603), quelled large-scale violence, and created stable and effective bureaucratic institutions.[30] However, the Western "opening" of Japan—in 1853 at the hands of Commodore Matthew Perry—critically damaged the Tokugawa regime's prestige and perceived efficacy.[31] Western influence altered the social dynamic in Japan, which, in combination with the widely accepted domestic dissatisfaction with the shogunate's ability to protect Japan from outside encroachment, led factions to challenge the shogun in favor of restoring supreme Japanese rule to the emperor. Those who sought to overthrow Tokugawa, primarily from the Satsuma and Choshu feudal domains, rose in numbers and resolve and waged war against Tokugawa, culminating in the Boshin Civil War (1867–69). In the face of mounting opposition, Tokugawa Yoshinobu—the last shogun—abdicated political power to Emperor Meiji. Those who died for political reformation from the national crisis in 1853 through the Boshin Civil War provided the impetus for Emperor Meiji to erect a shrine in honor of their sacrifice.[32]

Originally constructed as *Shokonsho* in 1869 by order of Emperor Meiji, the shrine was renamed in 1879 to reflect its present day title: Yasukuni. At Yasukuni, the souls of over 2.4 million *kami* are enshrined. Often compared to Western national cemeteries, Yasukuni is the place where Japan's war dead are remembered. Different from a cemetery, though, no remains of the honored reside at Yasukuni—only the spirit of the *kami*. In fact, the only tangible remains of any of the enshrined are name cards,

---

[29] The term "shogunate" refers to the ruling elite in Japan whereby the shogun—the military general whom the emperor charged with maintaining order throughout the realm—dominated all aspects of political, social, economic, and military affairs in Japan. See James McClain, *Japan: A Modern History* (New York: W.W. Norton, 2002), 5.

[30] McClain, *Japan*, 17–18.

[31] On 31 March 1854, Commodore Perry and shogunal representatives concluded the Treaty of Peace and Amity between the U.S. and Japan, which ended Japan's seclusion policy and lead to broader outside intrusion by Russia, France, and Britain with similar unequal treaties in 1856. See McClain, *Japan,* 138.

[32] In this context, Yasukuni has a dual purpose: (1) a Shinto shrine to worship *kami*, and (2) to honor those who died wresting power from the shogunate to restore it to the emperor.

which distorts the popular Western analogy that the Yasukuni Shrine is Japan's version of Arlington National Cemetery. The part of the analogy that does hold true is that, much like Arlington, Yasukuni is a place where Japanese can go to remember and honor those who died in service to their country.

## 2.   Enshrinement

The manner in which souls are interred merits a brief discussion. According to Ono, "the oldest and most prevalent type of the *kami*-faith is Shrine Shinto," which focuses on a nationalized shrine system.[33]   Shrines are served and presided over by priests. The Meiji Restoration saw the convergence of the institutions of church and state; priests became state officials and shrines became state institutions.[34]   In the immediate postwar order, however, the Supreme Commander for the Allied Powers (SCAP), General Douglas MacArthur, abolished state "sponsorship, support, perpetuation" and "financial support from public funds" of Shintoism with his 15 December 1945 "Shinto Directive."[35]   Following the disestablishment of state-sponsored Shinto, priests lost their official government status; however, the chief priests of post-1945 Shinto shrines were still responsible for interment activities, with respect to who is interred and when.[36]

As a final note on interment, once the chief priest enshrines a soul, that soul forever joins the *kami* and can never be separated. While a physical name card may be

---

[33] Ono, *Shinto*, 14.

[34] Ibid., 15, 41; The 1889 Japanese Constitution, which was bestowed upon the Japanese by Emperor Meiji, gave absolute power to the emperor. A popular contemporary argument (see William Sturgeon's *Japan's Yasukuni Shrine: Place of Peace or Place of Conflict*, page 38) is that the 1889 constitution made the emperor the head Shinto priest. However, no such language is explicitly stated in the constitution. Since the constitution endows the emperor with near absolute power, one might presume that the emperor could be the head priest, but such a conclusion is not supported by the document.

[35] The directive served as a point of departure for the much broader freedom of religion article found in the 1946 Japanese constitution. See "The Shinto Directive," In *Contemporary Religions in Japan* 1, no. 2 (1960): 85.

[36] Chief priests can only enshrine souls that can be named. Unidentifiable remains of those who died in service to Japan cannot be enshrined at Yasukuni. According to William Sturgeon, the Ministry of Health and Welfare (MHW) provides basic information (name, date and place of birth, and circumstances of death) on those considered for enshrinement to the chief priests. Thus the chief priests make the final determination on enshrinement, but the MHW determines who qualifies as war dead. See William Sturgeon, *Japan's Yasukuni Shrine: Place of Peace or Place of Conflict?* (Boca Raton: Dissertation.com, 2006), 66–67.

easily removed, the spirits of those venerated souls become intertwined in a non-physical plane and will remain as such forever.

### 3.    Politicization of Yasukuni

To understand why Yasukuni elicits the reactions it does among international audiences requires an appreciation of the finer points of the Yasukuni controversy. What is it about Yasukuni that so alarms Chinese and Koreans in ways absent other Shinto shrines? And has it always been this way? To answer these questions one must look beyond Yasukuni's dual purpose and explore the history of Yasukuni in regards to three politically charged issues: (1) Japanese prime minister visits to the shrine, (2) the capacity of those visits (official or private), and (3) the enshrinement of fourteen Class-A war criminals.

#### a.    *Prime Minister Visits to Yasukuni*

Even in postwar Japan, Yasukuni continued to thrive under its dual purpose of Shinto shrine and national war memorial, enshrining over two million from the Greater East Asian War (World War II).[37] Additionally, up through the early 1980s, it was commonplace for Japanese prime ministers to visit Yasukuni and pay tribute to their ancestors without causing diplomatic crises. Only after 1983 were these visits met with international outrage.

Since the signing of the San Francisco Peace Treaty with Allied powers in 1951, Japanese prime ministers visited the Yasukuni Shrine 64 times (see Table 1). The majority of these visits (67 percent) occurred in conjunction with the annual spring and autumn festivals at Yasukuni; ten visits occurred in mid-August commemorations of the end of the Pacific War (the first of which occurred in 1975) and eleven visits occurred outside of either the festivals or August.[38] While this study presents findings and analysis on the visits writ large in later chapters, it is worth taking note now of two Japanese prime ministerial friction points in the Yasukuni chronology that most modern

---

[37] Sturgeon, *Japan's Yasukuni Shrine,* 64.

[38] The annual spring and autumn festivals hold special significance to the Japanese. Prior to 1978, the Emperor of Japan, or his delegate, regularly attended these festivals.

scholarship focuses on: Prime Minster Nakasone Yasuhiro's 1985 visit and Prime Minister Koizumi Junichiro's 2001 visit.

Until 1983, the international community—notably China and South Korea—largely ignored Japanese prime minister visits to Yasukuni. Japanese Prime Minister Nakasone Yasuhiro broke that pattern when he visited on 15 August 1983 to commemorate 38th anniversary of the end of the Pacific War, prompting China to respond. Interestingly though, modern scholarship on the Yasukuni controversy credits Nakasone's 15 August 1985 visit as the event that first introduced international notoriety on the controversy. However, three issues of the *People's Daily* (16, 19, and 21 August 1983) detailing Beijing's official objection to Nakasone's 1983 visit discredit this conventional wisdom. Why the 1983 visit suddenly elicited such a response in ways previous visits did not remains unclear. What is clear is that, despite the August 1983 protest, Beijing's response to future Japanese prime minister visits was not consistent— neither in regards to future mid-August visits, nor to the visits more broadly. (The details of these inconsistencies are discussed later in the study.) While Nakasone's 1985 visit received intense Chinese criticism (such that it would be eleven years before another Japanese prime minister would visit), it was not the first time that Beijing responded.

In 2001, Koizumi Junichiro became the Japanese prime minister. Upon election to office, Koizumi pledged to visit Yasukuni on 15 August to honor those who died in service to Japan, thus wasting no time gaining Beijing and Seoul's attention. Koizumi visited Yasukuni as promised, though on the 13th rather than the 15th.[39] The visit marked the first time a Japanese prime minister visited Yasukuni in mid-August since Nakasone's last visit in 1985, and the visit set a precedence for Sino-Japanese relations for the whole of Koizumi's term. Despite repeated official objections from both Seoul and Beijing, Koizumi proceeded with annual visits to Yasukuni. Koizumi tried to mitigate the international tension these visits created by offsetting the timing of his 2003 and 2004 visits to January, but his efforts had little effect. The six visits during Koizumi's

---

[39] In an attempt to manage the inflammatory situation Koizumi's pledge created, Beijing secretly negotiated with Tokyo prior to August 2001 and both sides agreed that Koizumi would visit Yasukuni, but only after the sensitive World War II anniversary had passed. Koizumi, likely in an effort to appease domestic audiences, decided to ignore this agreement and visited Yasukuni on 13 August 2001, rather than wait until after the anniversary. See Ed Griffith, "The Three Phases of China's Response to Koizumi and the Yasukuni Shrine Issue: Structuration in Sino-Japanese Relations," *European Research Center on Contemporary Taiwan Online Paper Series* (2012), 12.

term, including his last visit on 15 August 2006, marked the nadir in Japan's postwar diplomatic relations with China and South Korea.

### b. *Capacity of Prime Minister Visits*

The question of whether the visits to the shrine were done in an official or unofficial capacity added a new wrinkle in the Yasukuni debate. At issue is the postwar separation of church and state and the constitutionality of prime ministers visiting Yasukuni, or any shrine for that matter, in their official capacity as prime minister. In keeping with MacArthur's Shinto directive, Article 20 of the 1946 Japanese Constitution prohibits governmental participation in any religious activity.[40] While Yasukuni is the place where Japan's war dead are honored, it is also a shrine. The debate in Japan, and elsewhere, is that Yasukuni's religious foundations cause the provisions of the Shinto directive and Article 20 of the constitution to apply. In this context, Japanese prime ministers could be prohibited from visiting Yasukuni in their official capacity, as defined by any prime minister signing the Yasukuni entry ledger with his or her title, driving to the shrine in a government vehicle, or paying for wreaths with public funds.

Aside from the constitutionality debate, the larger international community takes offense to official prime minister visits because of the symbolism such visits convey. Again, the fear is the message that such visits transmit: An unrepentant Japan bent on returning to its militarist roots. Conventional wisdom on the Yasukuni problem holds that the reason Prime Minister Nakasone's 1985 visit was so controversial was because it was the first time that any visiting prime minister went in an official capacity. Conventional wisdom on this aspect of the infamous 1985 visit, however, is also wrong. (The 1985 visit and the reactions it generated are compared later in the study.)

### c. *Class-A War Criminals*

Of the many issues that complicate the Yasukuni controversy, perhaps none is more controversial than the enshrinement of fourteen Class-A war criminals at

---

[40] "Constitution of Japan," in Hugh Borton, *Japan's Modern Century* (New York: Ronald Press, 1955), 490–507.

Yasukuni.[41]  In May 1946, MacArthur, acting in his capacity as SCAP, convened the International Military Tribunal for the Far East (IMTFE) in Tokyo to promptly try and punish war criminals in the Far East. According to James McClain, the tribunals lasted more than two years and "indicted twenty-eight former high-ranking [Japanese] government and military leaders," and "the tribunal sent seven men to the gallows, including Doihara Kenji and the former prime ministers Hirota Koki and Tojo Hideki."[42]

Many in Japan did not accept the verdict of the IMTFE and attempted to have those executed and/or deceased war criminals enshrined at Yasukuni. In 1966, the Ministry of Health and Welfare provided a list of war dead—inclusive of fourteen Class-A war criminals—to the Yasukuni chief priest requesting their enshrinement. The priest, Tsukuba Fujimaro (former member of a branch of the Imperial family), understanding the political sensitivity of such a request, deferred interment. Tsukuba's sudden death in 1977 allowed a former Imperial Navy Luietenant Commander, Matsudaira Nagoyoshi, to assume the position of chief priest at Yasukuni. Since the final determination for who is enshrined rests with the chief priest, Matsudaira secretly enshrined the war criminals on 17 October 1978.[43]

The interment of war criminals at Yasukuni aggravated what was already a sensitive issue with those who suffered at the hands of Imperial Japan. The impact of the enshrinement was felt not only in neighboring Asian nations, but also within Japan, and at the highest levels. Prior to 1978, the emperor attended the annual festivals at Yasukuni, but after the enshrinement of the war criminals, the Showa Emperor never

---

[41] According to Article 5 of the IMTFE Charter, criminal acts were grouped into three categories, or classes: (a) Crimes against peace, (b) conventional war crimes, and (c) crimes against humanity. Those like former Prime Minister Tojo Hideki who planned and ordered the conduct of the war, were tried for crimes against peace, and those convicted of such crimes are, therefore, referred to as Class-A war criminals. See "Charter of the International Military Tribunal for the Far East," at The Avalon Project at the Yale Law School, last accessed on March 29, 2013, http://web.archive.org/web/19990222030537/http://www.yale.edu/lawweb/avalon/imtfech htm.

[42] The validity of the tribunals has been long debated. Some argue that the verdicts merely reflected MacArthur's desire for "victor's justice," especially given the fact that the United States was exempt from the trials, which is notable given President Harry Truman's decision to use the atomic bombs that caused "indiscriminate destruction of civilian life and property." See McClain, *Japan,* 535–36.

[43] Sturgeon, *Japan's Yasukuni Shrine,* 67–73; Phil Deans, "Diminishing Returns? Prime Minister Koizumi's Visits to the Yasukuni Shrine in the Context of East Asian Nationalisms," *East Asia* 24 (2007): 281.

returned to the shrine. After years of domestic criticism and international consternation, calls at the mass level in Japan have been made to the government and to Yasukuni to remove the Class A war criminals from the shrine. Those familiar with Shinto, however, understand that this is an impossible proposal. Since the Japanese presumably understand their dilemma, perhaps the suggestion of disenshrinement was made as an overture of good will to international audiences rather than a solution consistent with Shinto.

In this context, while the enshrinement of war criminals is perhaps the most contentious issue in the Yasukuni debate, it is but one aspect of a much larger political problem besetting Japan's regional relationships. Barring a workable solution to the enshrinement of Japan's imperialistic past, this problem will likely persist for the foreseeable future.

## C.    CONCLUDING REMARKS

The Yasukuni problem is complex, indeed, and one cannot appreciate the responses in Beijing and Seoul to Japanese prime ministerial visits without an understanding of the relevant history. To understand Yasukuni is to understand the Shinto way of life. Just as Shinto is more than just a faith, Yasukuni is more than just a shrine. Yasukuni's origins in the Meiji Restoration laid its war memorial foundation while Shinto provided its religious purpose. Those who died in service to Japan during that contentious period combined with World War II war criminals have cast Yasukuni in an odd light whereby it now represents the best and worst of Japan. That the shrine has become such a politically charged issue provides observers of the 64 Japanese prime ministerial visits since 1951 an opportunity to use this complex issue to analyze and assess governmental responses to them in China and South Korea.

THIS PAGE INTENTIONALLY LEFT BLANK

# III. POLITICAL SYSTEMS AND STATE LEADERSHIP

The focus of this thesis is the effect that different political systems have on governmental responses to Japanese prime minister visits to Yasukuni. To that end, one must have a clear understanding of what the term "political system" means and why it matters. By defining this term and demonstrating its applicability to the PRC and the ROK, the reader can then move into the case studies with an appreciation of the political context in both countries during the 64 Yasukuni visits. Thus the goal of this chapter is to define these ambiguous terms and then apply them to China and South Korea dating back to approximately 1950 (coincidently the same observed period of Japanese prime minister visits to Yasukuni).

## A. POLITICAL SYSTEMS

What does the term "political system" mean and why is it important to understand what system governs country? *Encyclopedia Britannica* defines a political system as, "the set of formal legal institutions that constitute a 'government' or a 'state.'"[44] While a political system includes the formal type of government, it also captures the unique informal variables of politics, economics, and culture that further define how countries implement their version of their chosen system. The typology of political systems falls into three groups: consolidated democracies, transitional democracies, and authoritarian regimes.[45] To these systems we now turn.

### 1. Consolidated Democracies

While neither of the countries in this study qualify as a consolidated democracy, it is helpful to define this particular system because it helps frame the other two. Consolidated democracies are *established* representative governments that abide by a minimum of accepted tenets of political democracy. Robert Dahl provides a list of seven criteria that define, at a minimum, what a democratic country should look like:

---

[44] *Encyclopedia Britannica*, online ed., s.v. "Political System."

[45] Mark Kesselman, et al., *Introduction to Comparative Politics* (New York: Houghton Mifflin Harcourt Publishing, 2009), 20–24.

27

1. Control over government decisions about policy is constitutionally vested in elected officials.
2. Elected officials are chosen in frequent and fairly conducted elections in which coercion is comparatively uncommon.
3. Practically all adults have the right to vote in the election of officials.
4. Practically all adults have the right to run for elective offices in the government, though age limits may be higher for holding office than for the suffrage.
5. Citizens have a right to express themselves without the danger of severe punishment on political matters broadly defined, including criticism of officials, the government, the regime, the socio-economic order, and the prevailing ideology.
6. Citizens have a right to seek out alternative sources of information. Moreover, alternative sources of information exist and are protected by law.
7. To achieve their various rights . . . citizens also have a right to form relatively independent associations or organizations, including independent political parties and interest groups.[46]

Important to note is that while consolidated democracies adhere to these institutions relatively consistently, they occasionally violate certain tenets. The key is that on the whole, they remain true to the core democratic principles and have done so for a sustained period of time.

Dahl's criteria are not a comprehensive list of democratic principles. Some political theorists advocate for the inclusion of additional conditions—such as a military that is subordinate to elected governmental control or the existence of a judiciary with powers independent of the executive and legislative branches—but these additions are helpful refinements that build on what Dahl outlined as the foundations of a democracy.

## 2. Transitional Democracies

The difference between consolidated and transitional democracies focuses on two criteria: (1) longevity or durability, and (2) the extent of their democratic practice. The first criterion focuses on time. How long has a country been a democracy? At issue is the likelihood that the government will reverse to whatever its precondition was. While no minimum time standard necessarily exists, it is the author's assertion that a country that

---

[46] Robert Dahl, *Dilemmas of Pluralist Democracy: Autonomy vs. Control* (New Haven: Yale University Press, 1982), 10–11.

has been practicing democracy for at least fifty years is likely to retain its core democratic principles. Countries with less than fifty years of democracy are no less likely to consolidate their political system, but they fall into a transitional category because their government has not weathered time and change to the extent needed for their democratic foundation to solidify.[47]

Secondly, the extent of a country's democratic practice determines whether the spirit of democracy is embraced or if the government merely adopted democratic trappings while retaining an authoritarian core. Two common ways transitional democracies might claim formal institutions of democracy while concealing other-than democratic practices is in elections and pluralism. Governments may hold elections but unduly influence their outcome through fear, intimidation, or persuasion. Alternatively, governments will hold free elections, but not necessarily fair elections—fair in that the opposition party stands a chance at winning. Postwar Japan serves as examples of such a case. From 1955 until 1993, Japan's Liberal Democratic Party dominated politics, making it essentially a one-party state. Mark Kesselman summarizes the difference between consolidated and transitional democracies well: "Compared to consolidated democracies, political authorities in transitional systems are much more likely to engage in corruption, control of the media, intimidation and violence against opponents, vote rigging, and other measures to make sure they get reelected."[48]

### 3.    Authoritarianism

The third type of political system, authoritarianism, is a system characterized by a high concentration of power in a single individual, a small group, or a single party or institution, such as the military. Fear, intimidation, censorship, and political repression define the character of authoritarian regimes. Such regimes take many forms, inclusive of communist party-states, theocracies, military governments, absolute monarchies, and personal dictatorships.[49]

---

[47] Kesselman, et al., *Introduction to Comparative Politics*, 22.

[48] Ibid.

[49] Ibid., 22–23.

Looking at authoritarian regimes, several characteristics emerge that suggest that authoritarianism is more than just failing to meet the items on the democratic checklist: Some authoritarian tenets of governance are polar opposites from those of a democratic form of government. Steven Levitsky and Luncan Way detail four arenas of democratic contestation that highlight the spirit of authoritarianism. The first is the electoral arena. In authoritarian regimes, the electoral process either does not exist or the ruling party dominates the electoral process through fear, intimidation, coercion, or persuasion to such a degree that the process becomes hollow and useless. The second arena is the legislative apparatus. Similar to the electoral process, a legislature either does not exist or is so thoroughly controlled by the regime that separation or conflict between the executive and legislative bodies is unthinkable. The third arena, the judiciary, is typically subordinated to the ruling party and is therefore subject to party influence. Lastly, and possibly most notable, is state control of the media. Levitsky and Way point out, "In most full-blown autocracies, the media are entirely state-owned, heavily censored, or systematically repressed."[50]

As a final note on today's authoritarian states, it is becoming increasingly evident that they may coexist indefinitely with meaningful democratic institutions. Many authoritarian governments have moved away from their rigid forms of governance in favor of adopting certain democratic institutions, such as elections or measured privatization of media, in response to popular demands for it at the mass level. While authoritarian regimes may incorporate democratic elements in their governance, they do not embrace the spirit or core principles of democracy. Consequently, they risk instability by attempting to maintain a delicate balancing act between freedom and control.

## B. THE PEOPLE'S REPUBLIC OF CHINA: POLITICAL SYSTEM AND STATE LEADERSHIP

The government in Beijing serves as an example of a regime that began and has remained fully authoritarian, and, over time, has adopted certain democratic trappings in

---

[50] Steven Levitsky and Luncan Way, "The Rise of Competitive Authoritarianism," in *Readings in Comparative Politics: Political Challenges and Changing Agendas*, ed. Mark Kesselman (Boston: Wadsworth CENGAGE Learning, 2010), 100; Levitsky and Way, "The Rise of Competitive Authoritarianism," 98–101.

response to public opinion; though this result has been decades in the making. The current political system in China dates back to 1949, but the roots of the Chinese state can be traced back to the early 20th century. Since the scope of this study is on Beijing's response to Japanese prime minister visits to Yasukuni Shrine, the analysis of China's political system need not reach farther than the Chinese Communist Party's establishment of the People's Republic.

Though the review of the PRC's political system focuses on the authoritarian aspect of governance from 1949 up to present day, the following analysis may be best broken down by three eras: Mao era authoritarianism (1949–1976), Deng era authoritarianism (1976–1989), and the post-Tiananmen era authoritarianism (1989-present). In this way, the analysis demonstrates how and why China is an authoritarian regime while also unveiling the impact of key state leadership on politics over the observable period of Yasukuni visits. The goal of such an analysis is to help the reader put Beijing's array of responses to Yasukuni into a Chinese domestic politics perspective. In so doing, the reader will better understand the unique political circumstances that Beijing was subject to, and how that differs from the South Korean context.

### 1.    Mao Era Authoritarianism

Following Japan's surrender in 1945, China was riven by civil war between Chiang Kai-shek's Nationalist Party (Kuomintang [KMT]) and Mao Zedong's Chinese Communist Party (CCP). In 1949, after years of fighting and unsuccessful attempts at a coalition government (sponsored by the United States and assisted by the Soviet Union), Mao's Communist forces decisively defeated Chiang's KMT-led regime. Alice Miller and Richard Wich note, "On 1 October 1949, Mao proclaimed the establishment of the People's Republic of China (PRC), while Chiang Kai-shek reestablished the Republic of China (ROC) in Taipei . . . Each regime claimed to the be the sole legitimate government of China, launching a contest over national sovereignty that persisted until the 1990s."[51]

---

[51] Alice Miller and Richard Wich, *Becoming Asia: Change and Continuity in Asian International Relations Since World War II* (Stanford: Stanford University Press, 2011), 30.

The division of territory and sovereignty had profound effects on the PRC, both internationally and domestically. From an international perspective, while the Communist revolution swept the nationalist off the mainland, it failed to change the United States's orientation of formal recognition. The United States continued to back Chiang and the KMT in Taiwan, recognizing the ROC as the legitimate government of China. Beijing, consequently, suffered in diplomatic and economic isolation until 1972, when conflict in Indochina and a changing geopolitical landscape motivated Washington to align with Beijing in balance of power politics against Moscow.[52]

Domestically, Mao sought to restore power and prestige to his new Republic, even at extreme cost. Said Kenneth Lieberthal of Mao, "Mao, in short, was a strong leader who would not shrink from bloodshed and sacrifice to reach his goals."[53] Mao's goals of governing China and promoting revolutionary change were mutually antagonistic, which caused intense turmoil in the 1960s and 1970s. To achieve his goals, Mao demanded supreme authority over the Party and the people, evidenced by the CCP's constitution that, in Frederick Teiwes's opinion, "granted [Mao] formal powers to act unilaterally [from the Party collective leadership] in certain instances."[54]

Mao Zedong was driven by ideology, and the Chinese society under Mao was captivated by his ideas, charisma, and legacy, which gave him great latitude to implement bold policy initiatives—policy initiatives possible only in an authoritarian setting. For Mao, socialism, or the continuing class struggle, under the tenets of Marxism-Leninism was the driving idea behind his actions. Mao's authoritative standing as Chairman of the

---

[52] The shifting international context and U.S.-China rapprochement of the early 1970s had profound effects on the PRCs international status. In 1971, Beijing took Taipei's seat at the United Nations—an epoch moment that signaled international recognition of sovereignty of the PRC. The following year saw Richard Nixon's historic visit to Beijing and the signing of the Shanghai Communiqué, which reduced the tension between the old antagonists and enabled them to enter into a new strategic relationship. The communiqué marked the beginning of the United States' rather ambiguous "one China" policy and also facilitated the establishment of diplomatic relations between China and Japan. Establishing diplomatic ties with the United States allowed the PRC to break out of isolation and join the Western-led international order. Therefore, it can be said that 1971 was the most important date in modern Chinese history. See Miller and Wich, *Becoming Asia,* 170–77.

[53] Kenneth Lieberthal, *Governing China: From Revolution through Reform* (New York: W.W. Norton, 2004), 59.

[54] Frederick Teiwes, "The Establishment and Consolidation of the New Regime, 1949–1957," in *The Politics of China*, ed. Roderick MacFarquhar (Cambridge: Cambridge University Press, 2011), 12.

CCP and his legacy as the founder of the communist revolution in China is what afforded him the ability to implement his ideology. Mao led China as Chairman for nearly three decades, and over that period there are myriad examples one could highlight to demonstrate the authoritarian context of the time, but such an effort would exceed the scope needed to prove the point. Instead, the study focuses three policy initiatives under Mao that showcase authoritarian rule under Mao: the Hundred Flowers Campaign, the Great Leap Forward, and the Great Proletarian Cultural Revolution.

In the wake of Soviet Premier Joseph Stalin's death in 1953, the Soviet Union under Nikita Khrushchev implemented reforms that sent off shock waves in the socialist camp. Known as "de-Stalinization," the convulsions of how to address the gross abuses of Stalin threatened the cohesion of the Soviet bloc, evidenced most acutely by autonomy movements from Moscow in Poland and Hungary in the mid-1950s. In the burgeoning Sino-Soviet schism, Mao learned from what he perceived as Khrushchev's mishandling of de-Stalinization and sought to avoid similar socialist clashes from occurring within China. The result was a "rectification campaign" aimed at addressing the roles of the rulers and the ruled in the Communist system. Of the Hundred Flowers campaign, Alice Miller and Richard Wich write:

> Mao permitted "a hundred flowers to bloom and a hundred schools of thought to contend," an invitation to the Chinese people to vent their grievances and criticize the regime for its shortcomings and faults. A deluge of criticism was unleashed, producing such a challenge to the regime that the campaign was cut short after less than six weeks.[55]

In this context, authoritarian characteristics of governance are clearly evident. Mao gave the freedom of speech to the people only to take it back sharply after the attendant criticism threatened that which he cherished most: power.

After the first Five-Year Plan expired (1953–1957), Mao sought a new strategy to improve China's economy and spearhead an initiative towards industrialization that built upon the successes of the previous plan while not exploiting the agricultural sector like the Soviet model recommended. For Mao, the Great Leap Forward (GLF) would serve as a catalyst towards a modern, industrialized, communist China. From 1958 through 1961,

---

[55] Miller and Richard Wich, *Becoming Asia*, 124.

33

the initiative ravaged the agrarian sector and resulted in calamity because Mao overestimated the power of mass mobilization and underestimated the time requirements to develop the factors of production to reach their full potential. The Great Leap caused rural starvation—perhaps the deadliest in human history—and, instead of advancing the economy, produced economic regression.[56] Mao's power and prestige suffered from the failure, but even though Mao's power declined, it is notable that the GLF began not because of Mao's power per se, but rather because of his visionary theory of China's future. Moreover, the GLF represents a radical policy of collectivization that would otherwise be untenable in other political systems.

The last thrust of authoritarian policy driven by Mao's ideology was the initiation of the Great Proletarian Cultural Revolution (GPCR) from 1966–1976. In what would all too easily be attributed as a power play by Mao to eliminate political rivals who rose from the ashes of the GLF, a closer examination reveals that the GPCR was an extreme policy initiative that reflected Mao's ideology of class struggle against the exploitative politicians and bureaucrats who fell out of touch with the people. Harry Harding asserts that in the early 1960s, Mao was dissatisfied with the policies that the Party was pursuing: "A return to private farming in agriculture, the resurrection of material incentives in industry, a concentration on urban medicine in public health, the development of a two-track system in education, and the reappearance of traditional themes and styles in literature and the arts."[57] These policies were, has Harding notes, "incompatible with his [Mao's] vision of a socialist society," compelling Mao to mobilize society to purify the party he helped create.[58]

The political conflict that ensued out of the GPCR was a byproduct of Mao's ideological differences with other Party elites. According to Harding, Mao deemed "'Party persons in authority' who might attempt to follow the capitalist road" as the

---

[56] Lieberthal, *Governing China*, xvi.

[57] Harry Harding, "The Chinese State in Crisis, 1966–1969," in *The Politics of China*, ed. Roderick MacFarquhar (Cambridge: Cambridge University Press, 2011), 151.

[58] Ibid.

greatest threat to the socialist revolution.[59] How Mao implemented his vision demonstrates the linkage between ideology, power, and policy. For Mao, the charismatic founder of the CCP who seemingly commanded the devotion of the Chinese, ideology was primary: a socialist revolution was needed. Mao then used his power to build the support base needed to carry out such an audacious plan. He bolstered his support base in the military through Lin Biao by politicizing the People's Liberation Army (PLA). Mao enlisted the support of radical intellectuals who propagated both criticisms of Mao's rivals and the ideology behind the GPCR. Lastly, Mao appealed to the mass student base, calling them to struggle against government leaders at all levels. The Cultural Revolution successfully muted Mao's rivals, as demonstrated by the removal of the top two CCP power holders: Liu Shaoqi and Deng Xiaoping. However, by attempting to prevent revisionism, Mao damaged the CCP's ability to resist economic modernization policies later on, which ultimately undermined the ideology behind the GPCR and brought about the economic and structural change Mao sought to repress.

Though Mao's endeavors ended up damaging domestic society and international prestige, his actions were driven by socialist ideological commitments, the same commitments that bore fruit during Mao's first revolution. Mao's image from the civil war and rather successful period from 1949–1957 afforded him the latitude to implement such bold policies. More broadly, though, they reflect the unique characteristics of authoritarian rule under China's famed leader.

## 2.    Deng Era Authoritarianism

After Mao passed in 1976, the PRC took on a new character but held true to its authoritarian foundation. Hua Guafeng succeeded Mao, but his tenure was short-lived. The central figure in Chinese politics after Mao was Deng Xiaoping. Deng, much like Mao, was a leader with strong ideological commitments, but Deng differed from Mao in focus: Mao's ideology focused on social revolution over economic progress while Deng's ideology focused on economic modernization over social revolution. Though Deng's pragmatic approach to Chinese modernization focused on rationale over socialist dogma,

---

[59] Ibid., 153.

his Marxist-Leninist commitments played the dominant role in policy formulation, and, because of his revolutionary achievements alongside Mao, he too commanded the respect from the masses. Those same commitments that compelled Deng to strengthen China's economic base drove the agriculture and economic reform policies that were not feasible under Mao.

After being twice purged from the CCP, Deng Xiaoping's struggle for power resulted in his becoming the leader of the PRC in 1978, and his ideology changed the Party's direction. His campaign for making practice the sole criteria for truth was aimed at the pursuit of economic policies that worked in practice (an implicit criticism of Mao's blind pursuit of failed policies). Deng firmly believed that economic development was the best way for China to advance towards the ideal communist state in keeping with Marxist-Leninist ideology, and that Mao's class struggle-centered policies were misguided.

Deng believed that China could tolerate capitalist economic methods to build its economic base while remaining true to socialism and, by doing so, China would progress in the initial stages, albeit for quite a while, to reach its full potential. In this context, Deng implemented agricultural and economic reforms that moved the Chinese economy away from its traditional command economy towards a market economy. These reforms helped grow the economy at nearly ten percent annually, but as the economy grew, so too did the unexpected political volatility of policy expansion and contraction through the 1980s. Yet that political volatility was a manifestation of Deng's belief in adjusting policy through practice. Throughout his tenure, his ideological commitments stood firm and his power allowed him to shape the country in accordance with his vision of China's future.

While Deng recognized that China needed to reform to advance with the modern industrialized world, he did not hesitate to leverage the control afforded him in an authoritarian system. Two examples highlight this tendency: the 1978–79 Democracy Wall movement and the Tiananmen protest movement. In 1977, Deng charged Hu Yaobang with the rehabilitation of those purged during the GPCR. A controversial topic for several reasons, not least of which being victims of the Cultural Revolution working alongside their former accusers, Hu energetically led efforts to correct as many Party wrongs as possible. Rehabilitating the purged undermined the logic of the GPCR, an initiative Hua Guafeng sought to defend. The political space that Hu's effort generated led to protests. Protestors arguing for a wide range of issues posted their proclamations on what became known as Democracy Wall, which quickly got the attention of Party leadership. Deng initially supported the movement because it helped him wrest power from Hua, but his short-term gains cost him in the long-run. The protests shifted in focus from the despotism of Mao to dictatorship in China more broadly (a threat to the regime), with activists demanding democracy. In 1979, Deng, who had never favored democracy, put an end to Democracy Wall and imprisoned key political activists.[60]

The 1989 Tiananmen protest demonstrates the depth of power and control that authoritarian regimes wield. Characteristic of regime governance under Deng was an oscillation of policy reform and retrenchment. The year 1985 saw a surge of policy reform, notably in science, technology, and urban economics. These reforms, championed by Hu Yaobang (architect of the Commission for Sino-Japanese Friendship in the Twenty-first Century), created economic winners and losers in China. In 1986, when the policy pendulum swung back, popular demand forced Deng to remove Hu from his post. The next cycle of policy volatility in 1987 and 1988 divided the Party to such an extent that calamity was all but a certainty. The sudden death of Hu Yaobang in 1989 sparked student protests, calling on the Party to recognize the merits of the purged reformer. The demonstrations over Hu grew and shifted in focus to the regime itself. Facing mounting opposition, on 3 June 1989 Deng and his colleagues ordered the PLA to intervene. The action resulted in thousands of civilians killed and wounded for exercising their freedom of speech defined in Article 35 of the Chinese Constitution.[61]

---

[60] Lieberthal, *Governing China,* 135–37.

[61] Ibid., 139–44; "The Common Program of the Chinese People's Political Consultative Conference," (1949), last accessed April 3, 2013, http://e-chaupak.net/database/chicon/1949/1949e.pdf; "The Constitution of the People's Republic of China," (2004), last accessed April 3, 2013, http://www.npc.gov.cn/englishnpc/Constitution/node_2825.htm.

### 3.    Post-Tiananmen Authoritarianism

Though Beijing recovered in certain aspects from the Tiananmen tragedy, the event set the precedent for Chinese state-society relationships. The memory of the massacre lingers on, both for any would-be opposition movements and for the regime itself. For Chinese citizens, they understand the political context in which they exist: play by the rules or suffer the consequences. For the regime, they realize that intra-Party division creates opportunities that the masses can exploit. The somewhat tacit state-society social contract is particularly important with regard to China's Japan policy. Japanese provocations, such as prime minister visits to Yasukuni, generate swells of anti-Japanese nationalism at the mass level to which the Party must respond. Both participants, the regime and the masses, understand that each has limits to how far they can push their agenda. The regime knows that if they are not responsive to public opinion they risk national uprising reminiscent to Tiananmen. The people, on the other hand, know that if they protest beyond the regime's limits of dissent, they risk harsh suppression. The delicate balancing act constrains China's Japan policy and frustrates the fragile state-society relationship.

Post-Tiananmen China has witnessed the adoption of many democratic institutions while retaining its authoritarian foundation. Regarding the role of the military, just as largely as the PLA was politicized under Mao, Jiang Zemin (General Secretary of the CCP, 1989–2002) decoupled the military from politics, making it subordinate to state leadership.[62] Regarding elections, while the PRC is a one-party state, elections are held down to the local level, and leaders are accountable to their constituencies in that they can be replaced with another Party nominee for poor performance. At the highest levels, China is reforming its electoral processes by allowing each Party congress to elect its leadership at its own territorial level rather than rely on the legacy *nomenklatura* appointments (Soviet-style list of leading positions, candidates, and rules, all of which the Party controls).[63]    The regime has also relaxed its

---

[62] The chairman of the Central Military Commission (China's supreme military command organization)—currently the general secretary of the CCP and PRC president—is appointed by the CCP Central Committee and directs the activities of the Chinese armed forces.

[63] Lieberthal, *Governing China,* 234, 242.

control/censorship over the media and the Internet, though the Party exercises control over these to prevent uncontrolled access to information from leading to chaos.

For all these reasons, the PRC is clearly an authoritarian state. The PRC has been and continues today to be a one-party state. China under Mao was characterized by a commanding figure that enjoyed the political latitude to engage or ignore domestic or international stimuli (as in the case of Yasukuni) consistent with socialist principles. China under Deng focused on economic advances to guide its foreign and domestic policy. While post-Tiananmen China has adopted some trappings of democracy, they are merely window dressing for what is still—and will be for the foreseeable future—a thoroughly authoritarian regime.

## C. THE REPUBLIC OF KOREA: POLITICAL SYSTEM AND STATE LEADERSHIP

The ROK presents a useful case study for this thesis, for over the observed period the ROK started out authoritarian but then democratized in 1988. The change of political system lends credibility in both the findings of Seoul's response to Yasukuni, but also in comparison to Beijing's. How authoritarian South Korea responded versus how democratizing South Korea responded is important and makes the comparison to itself and to another authoritarian state useful. The following analysis outlines the ROK's authoritarian beginnings and its transition to democracy.

### 1. Authoritarian South Korea (1948–1988)

The end of Japanese occupation of the Korean peninsula in 1945 left the country divided at the 38th parallel, with the United States administering the southern territory and the Soviet Union administering the north. After attempts to hold peninsula-wide elections failed, the two nation-states of South Korea and North Korea were created in 1948. Within two years and after the departure of both Soviet and United States forces, the peninsula became embroiled in civil war that ravaged the Korean people and territory. The Korean War exacted a heavy toll on the ROK, decimating the South Korean economy and infrastructure. In response to the heavy burden of rebuilding a war-torn nation, the South Korean leadership took on a decidedly authoritarian character for the proceeding four decades. Thus, this section focuses on three regimes: Rhee Syngman, Park Chung-hee, and Chun Doo-hwan.

In 1948, Rhee Syngman became the first president of the ROK. Beset by the division of the Korean peninsula and internal strife over the residual American occupation, Rhee struggled to build a state out of the impoverished country he inherited. Rhee had long desired to lead South Korea and, once installed as its leader, was quick to stamp out any resistance movements to his rule (primarily from the ROK political left). Rhee's brutal suppression of Communist and other opposition movements set South Korea on an authoritarian footing. Before any serious economic initiatives got off the ground, though, war visited his country once again, and the devastation of its aftermath left Rhee with more challenges than when he first took office. Bruce Cumings summarizes the general atmospherics of 1950s South Korea well: "South Korea in the 1950s was a terribly depressing place, where extreme privation and degradation touched everyone."[64]

Despite Rhee's significant exposure to democracy in the United States during his self-initiated exile during the Japanese occupation (1904–10; 1912–45), the fratricidal conflict only exacerbated Rhee's proclivity towards authoritarianism. Rhee's political suppression continued in the post-conflict years as did his intolerance for opposition. In an effort to solidify his position of power, Rhee engaged in crony capitalism, giving state patronage to the various *chaebol* in exchange for political support.[65] By rigging elections in 1956 and 1960, Rhee dominated domestic politics until widespread reform movements in 1960 forced his resignation.[66]

---

[64] Bruce Cumings, *Korea's Place in the Sun: A Modern History* (New York: W.W. Norton, 2005), 303.

[65] "Chaebol" refers to the large, family-owned business conglomerates that exercise monopolistic or oligopolistic control over various business sectors. According to Cummings, Rhee gave low purchase prices on former Japanese industries to chaebol in exchange for political support. The owner of Samsung, Yi Pyong-chol, for example, was accused of providing 64 million won to Rhee's party. See Cumings, *Korea's Place in the Sun,* 306–08, 326–27.

[66] "Syngman Rhee," *The Cold War Files*, The Wilson Center, last accessed April 8, 2013, http://legacy.wilsoncenter.org/coldwarfiles/index-33794.html.

The period of Rhee's tenure (1948–1960) marked a low point in ROK-Japan relations. Rhee harbored deep distrust and animosity towards the Japanese: It was the Japanese that occasioned his 33-year exile. As such, South Koreans under Rhee's influence remained intransigent and contemptuous towards Japan, making normalization impossible at the time. However, the political context between the ROK and Japan changed after Rhee was deposed.

As concentrated as political power was in Rhee, it pales in comparison to Korea's next autocratic leader, Park Chung-hee. In 1961, following the political turmoil in Rhee's wake, Major General Park led a military junta that toppled the ROK transitional government. Park's forceful seizure of power meant that he had much more freedom of action in regards to policy initiatives and governance if not the latitude to completely ignore public opinion. Unlike Rhee who was vindictive against the Japanese, Park was a pragmatist who saw Japan's economic success as a model to emulate. Park, however, had to persuade South Koreans that normalizing relations with Japan was necessary for economic improvement—an immensely unpopular proposition.

From the moment Park took power, he sought to improve relations with Japan, even at considerable cost. Park, a noted "Japanophile" whose military career was nurtured by the Japanese during the occupation, pursued normalization for several years after taking office.[67] In 1965 the two nations normalized relations, resulting in an emotional explosion amongst large segments of South Korea against Park.[68] Not one to

---

[67] According to Lee Chong-sik, Park was a graduate of the "Manchukuo and Japanese military academies and a first lieutenant in the Japanese army." See Lee Chong-sik, *Japan and Korea: The Political Dimension* (Stanford: Hoover Institution Press, 1985), 45.

[68] The 1965 Treaty on Basic Relations between Japan and the Republic of Korea normalized diplomatic relations and included a separate settlement on property and claims—war reparations—that totaled $800 million ($300 million in Japanese grants, $200 million in government loan from the Overseas Development Aid fund, and $300 million in commercial loans). Koreans viewed the settlement as dismally low and the treaty as renewed Japanese economic and political exploitation. See Lee, *Japan and Korea,* 54–55; "Treaty on Basic Relations between Japan and the Republic of Korea," *Database of Japanese Politics and International Relations,* Institute of Oriental Culture, University of Tokyo, last accessed April 8, 2013, http://www.ioc.u-tokyo.ac.jp/~worldjpn/documents/texts/docs/19650622.T1E.html; "Agreement Between Japan and the Republic of Korea Concerning the Settlement of Problems in regard to Property and Claims and Economic Co- Operation," *International Legal Materials* 5, no. 1 (1966): 111–117.

tolerate opposition, Park ordered the ROK army and police to suppress protesters. The 28 August 1965 FBIS *Daily Report* describes Park's actions:

> Immediately after a secret conference of Pak Chong-hui [sic] and military leaders, an ROK division was moved into Seoul from the demilitarized zone. The division is [sic] armed with tanks and armored cars. Demonstrators were beaten at random by troops, and on 26 August about 150 persons were wounded and 280 demonstrators were arrested.[69]

Park's vision of a secure Republic hinged on economic prosperity, as enunciated in his famous dictum, "Rich country, strong army."[70] By assiduously investing in heavy industrialization, Park, through the chaebol, achieved economic takeoff. Park's industrialization initiative, "the Big Push," built up areas of South Korea of his choosing, while ignoring rural development elsewhere.[71] In so doing, Park sowed the seeds of economic inequality that both he and his successor would reap. While Park engaged in economic winner-picking, the Korean economy writ large benefitted from his initiatives. By 1990, the South Korean economy was growing at nearly 10 percent annually, with low inflation (2–5 percent) and unemployment (2–4 percent), all driven by Park's one-party regime.[72] The period from 1961–1979 can therefore be characterized as intense focus on improving the ROK's security through economic prosperity—a major factor in the Yasukuni analysis.

In 1979, for reasons unknown, Kim Chae-gyu, chief of the Korean Central Intelligence Agency, murdered Park. The ensuing political upheaval set the conditions for the emergence of another military regime under Major General Chun Doo-hwan. Quickly seizing the political initiative, Chun dissolved the National Assembly and all political parties, and established a state of martial law to quell domestic tension. The response was

---

[69] Moscow in Korean to Korea, August 28, 1965, in FBIS *Asia*, August 30, 1965, BB12.

[70] Cumings, *Korea's Place in the Sun,* 317.

[71] The Big Push was program of heavy and chemical industrialization focused on the development of six sectors: steel, automobiles, chemicals, shipbuilding, machine tools, and electronics. The preponderance of chaebol receiving state patronage were those in or near Park's hometown. See Cumings, *Korea's Place in the Sun,* 322–26.

[72] Cumings, *Korea's Place in the Sun,* 340.

not well received, and opposition movements in the Cholla province—an area the Big Push left behind—tested the resolve of Chun's so-called democracy.

On 18 May 1980, hundreds of protestors took to the streets in Kwangju demanding an end to the martial law enacted by Chun earlier that year. In response, Chun ordered elite paratroopers into Kwangju to suppress the movement. "Paratroopers . . . landed in the city and began the indiscriminate murder of students, women, children—anyone who got in their way," notes Bruce Cumings.[73] Thousands died in Kwangju, and, similarly to Tiananmen, these people supposedly enjoyed Constitutional provisions of freedom of speech and assembly. Chun blamed the Kwangju incident on political dissident Kim Dae-jung—Park Chung-hee's chief rival who, by this time, had become the political vanguard of Cholla Province. The persecution of Kim would have implications on ROK-Japan relations later in the 1980s.[74]

In February 1981, Chun inaugurated himself president. Yet, even as president he continued his repressive tactics, likely in an effort to mimic the climate Park Chung-hee commanded. Chun "purged or proscribed the political activities of 800 politicians and 8,000 officials in government and business," and imprisoned some "37,000 journalists, students, teachers, labor organizers, and civil servants into 'purification camps,'" according to Bruce Cumings.[75] In the mid-1980s, Chun vastly increased the size of paramilitary riot police, whose charter it was to suppress demonstrations. Rather than consolidate his power base, Chun's brutal tactics drove what little support he had away, thus setting the stage for political reform.

---

[73] Ibid., 382.

[74] Kim Dae-jung had a large impact on Korean politics, dating back to 1971. The complexity of Kim's political activity dramatically impacted ROK-Japan relations throughout the 1980s, to include the calibration of Korean policy towards Japanese prime minister visits to the Yasukuni Shrine, as well as the ROK's transition to democracy. Bruce Cumings notes, "[Kim] was run over by a truck in 1971, kidnapped in 1973, put under house arrest until 1979, indicted in 1980 on trumped-up charges of having fomented the Kwangju Rebellion and nearly executed until the Carter and Reagan administrations . . . jointly intervened in late 1980, exiled to the United States in 1982, returned to house arrest again in 1985, and finally able to run in the 1987 direct presidential elections, only to lose when the opposition once again split and Kim Young Sam ran against him, thus electing Roh Tae Woo with a little over one-third of the vote. Kim's mass appeal sharply transformed Korea's pattern of authoritarianism and elite democracy." Quoted from Cummings, *Korea's Place in the Sun*, 366.

[75] Cummings, *Korea's Place in the Sun*, 384.

## 2.    Democratization (1988-present)

The democratization movement in the ROK had been fomenting since the days of Park Chung-hee, but became peculiarly acute in the mid-1980s. By 1985, Chun had become increasingly unpopular, and the opposition movement waited for the right opportunity to mobilize. The 24th Olympiad in Seoul proved to be the catalyst for change.

In 1985, South Korean society, tired by decades of military regimes, sought to end the perpetuation of military regime dominance and pressed for a constitutional amendment allowing direct presidential elections. In the face of mounting opposition, Chun—mindful of the coming Olympic games—agreed to support constitutional change and also agreed to leave office at the end of his term in 1988. Chun, however, preferred to pick his successor so that he could hold on to power from behind the scenes. In April 1987, after waiting for a break in the democratic momentum, Chun reversed his decision to support constitutional change. Chun quickly nominated his trusted colleague Roh Tae-woo to succeed him, knowing that Roh would easily dominate elections in an authoritarian setting.

The country erupted in protests. Knowing that any implementation of martial law similar to Kwangju would jeopardize the Olympics and thus embarrass the ROK on the international stage, protestors used this constraint to their advantage and pressed for political reform. Rather than scuttle the Olympiad, Roh split with Chun in June 1987 and agreed to free and fair presidential elections. The December 1987 presidential elections ended authoritarianism in the ROK, ushering in a new era of transitional democracy.[76]

Since 1988, the ROK has retained strong democratic underpinnings that appear durable. Free and fair national elections have occurred every five years for the presidency, to include election of the first opposition party nominee in 1998, Kim Dae-jung. Unlike the previous military regimes that could leverage the autocratic tools of censorship or violence to steer public opinion, elected officials must be responsive to

---

[76] Chalmers Johnson, "South Korean Democratization: The Role of Economic Development," *The Pacific Review* 2, no.1 (1989): 8.

public opinion. For all intents and purposes, the ROK seems to have shed its authoritarian skin in favor of representative government, but only time will tell.

## D.     CONCLUDING REMARKS

Political systems can reveal much about what can be expected from a government in terms of response to certain stimuli and how that response is implemented. With regard to Yasukuni, one might expect a democracy to react differently than an authoritarian regime because a representative government must be responsive to public demand whereas authoritarian regimes can ignore or suppress public opinion with impunity. To discover why the central governments in the PRC and ROK responded in the manner they did to Japanese prime minister visits to Yasukuni demands a clear understanding of the system within which each operates. In China, the authoritarian rule the People's Republic was founded in persists to this day. Veteran revolutionaries like Mao and Deng implemented bold policy initiatives with varying degrees of success, and both leveraged draconian measures to reign in public opinion when the desired outcome was not achieved. Today, Beijing finds itself balancing between political liberalization and control over the populace. Calls for political liberalization cannot be completely ignored, yet regime survival is the leadership's top priority. How Beijing reconciles what would appear to be mutually antagonistic outcomes will be interesting to observe.

In the ROK, post-conflict conditions demanded an approach for which authoritarianism seemed the best fit. Years of political persecution, corruption, and ineffective economic reform under Rhee led to a national uprising that left a void that the military filled. The first military regime under Park Chung-hee, while brutal, steered South Korea towards economic prosperity. The second military regime under Chun Doo-hwan tried to mimic the achievements of the Park regime, but came up short and instead distanced the regime from the public. In their pursuit of political reform, South Koreans leveraged unique conditions to set the ROK on a democratic footing. The successful transition to democracy led to many significant political changes, not the least of which being demands for response to Japanese provocations.

With the foundation for the study explained, we now turn to the case studies to see how the political systems in both countries impacted the observed responses to the Yasukuni Shrine.

# IV. BEIJING'S RESPONSE TO JAPANESE PRIME MINISTER VISITS TO YASUKUNI

Since the founding of the People's Republic in 1949, Japanese prime ministers have been visiting the Yasukuni Shrine, and Beijing's response to these visits has varied from ignoring them to lodging state objection to them, and degrees in between. The purpose of this chapter is to measure Beijing's observable response to each of the 64 prime ministerial visits to Yasukuni and determine what patterns exist and why. To this end, a chronological approach of the visits from 1951 to present day establishes what the government in Beijing did, if anything, in response to each visit. Where no observable response existed, Beijing's motivations for ignoring visits are assessed in the context of prevailing Sino-Japanese bilateral relations. Beijing's responses are thus graded as either ignoring the visit or responding to it with any type of official objection to the visit itself (not to Yasukuni in general). Since state leadership affects the character of the government, the following analysis follows a chronology that mirrors the PRC section of the previous chapter.

The argument advanced in this chapter is that up 1982, China largely ignored Japanese prime ministerial visits to Yasukuni. Between 1982 and 1985, Beijing reversed the pattern of previous decades, but was inconsistent in its responses. The trend through the mid-1990s and the 2000s is of increasing and consistent objection. A recurring theme revealed in all of Beijing's responses is clear: China wishes to discourage Japan from returning to its militaristic past.

## A. YASUKUNI VISITS DURING THE MAO ERA

Mao served as the chairman of the CCP from the founding of the PRC in 1949 until his death in 1976. During his tenure, six Japanese prime ministers visited Yasukuni Shrine thirty times (nearly half of all Yasukuni visits over the rated period). No evidence was found to support the claim that Beijing lodged an official protest over any of these visits. But that is not to say that the Yasukuni Shrine and its attendant symbolism did not resonate in Beijing during this period. With no observable responses or published policy with which to definitively prove Beijing's position on the matter, however, one must look at bilateral relations to explain why over the longest stretch the Beijing leadership ignored so many visits—the same kind of visits that caused passionate swells of anti-Japanese nationalism later on. A review of the bilateral relations under each Japanese prime minister reveals some possible explanations.

One characteristic of the PRC government under Mao worth noting is the victorious historic narrative of the People's Republic. Mao led the Communist revolution that defeated the imperialist Japanese and the Kuomintang, and his rhetoric of Chinese strength defined much of Chinese foreign policy throughout this period. Relations with the Japanese from 1949 through 1976 are indicative of this historic narrative.[77]

### 1. Yoshida Shigeru (1948–1954)

Prime Minister Yoshida, Japan's first prime minister after the American occupation, visited Yasukuni five times. All five visits occurred during the spring and autumn festivals. The first three visits (18 October 1951, 17 October 1952, and 23 April 1953) occurred against the backdrop of the Korean War (25 June 1950 - 27 July 1953), and, more specifically, after Chinese People's Volunteer intervention in November 1950. In the context of such a violent and complicated conflict, it is reasonable to conclude that the visit of Japan's prime minister to the Yasukuni Shrine might not register as high as it might during more peaceful conditions.

On the other hand, in light of the San Francisco treaty, Mao had some incentive to rally popular opinion against Japan in 1951. The peace treaty Yoshida signed on 8 September 1951 was not signed by the People's Republic of China (nor the Republic of China, for that matter). Mao could have easily made issue of Yoshida's visit to Yasukuni, if for nothing more than to bring awareness of China's exclusion from the peace treaty and foment anti-Japanese fervor. Similarly, Mao took no observable issue with Yoshida's

---

[77] Given China's low economical standing and its precarious geostrategic location respective of the two superpowers (the United States and the Soviet Union) from 1950s though the late 1970s, Beijing saw itself as weak and vulnerable. For this reason, Beijing's rhetoric was that it was strong and powerful. Beijing's bold economic initiatives (the Great Leap) and relocating its defense industrial sector deep within the interior (third front) over the same period attest to this reality.

1952 Yasukuni visit, which came not even six months after Japan entered into a peace treaty with the Republic of China—effectively barring any chance of entering into the same with the PRC. Beijing could have protested Yoshida's visit as a proxy for dissatisfaction with Tokyo's de facto recognition of Taipei, yet they did not. Both events suggest that Yasukuni did not rate high enough for Mao to respond to in any meaningful way.

## 2.    Kishi Nobusuke (1957–1960)

Prime Minister Kishi Nobusuke was the next Japanese prime minister to go to Yasukuni after Yoshida, visiting twice: once in the spring of 1957 and again in the fall of 1958.[78] While neither visit elicited a response from Beijing, it should be noted that the state of affairs between China and Japan under Kishi can be characterized as one of crisis, which begs the question why Beijing ignored an opportunity to criticize Tokyo. From the onset of his tenure as prime minister, Kishi's past service in the wartime regime and present pro-Taiwan inclinations alarmed Beijing.[79] In June 1957, after merely five months in office (and only two months after visiting Yasukuni), Kishi conducted a 15-day good-will tour of six Southeast Asian countries, culminating in a visit to Taiwan—making Kishi the first Japanese prime minister to visit the ROC. While Beijing did not object to Kishi's Southeast Asia tour, his visit to Taipei angered regime leadership and set China on an anti-Kishi footing. Premier Zhou Enlai described the political climate well: "This [visit to Taiwan] made the Chinese people angry. In other words, Premier Kishi's behavior in Taiwan has antagonized 600 million Chinese people."[80] Sino-Japanese relations deteriorated from the remainder of Kishi's tenure.

Adding to the troubled ties between China and Japan was the forthcoming revision of the U.S.-Japanese security treaty. Beijing was concerned that Kishi would

---

[78] For reasons unknown, Prime Ministers Hatoyama Ichiro (1954–56) and Ishibashi Tanzan (1956–57) did not pay tribute at the shrine. Both prime ministers were renowned for their efforts to build relationships with the PRC. Their combined tenure spanned the majority of the PRC's very successful first five-year plan. The early success Mao enjoyed from 1953–57 might have distracted him enough from Yasukuni even if either of Kishi's predecessors had visited, but this is mere speculation.

[79] Reference to Kishi's affiliation with the wartime regime from Miller and Wich, *Becoming Asia*, 61.

[80] Peking, Chinese International Service, July 25, 1957, in FBIS *Asia*, July 26, 1957, AAA6.

accentuate Japan's security ties to the United States and extend Japan's power in Taiwan and Southeast Asia.[81] Sino-Japanese ties reached a nadir in 1958 when China ceased all trade and exchanges with Japan. On 2 May, as Chinese tempers flared with regard to Kishi's pro-Taiwan stance, an incident at a Nagasaki department store involving a Japanese disgracing a PRC flag provided Beijing the opportunity to take punitive action against Japan for Kishi's support to Taiwan under the auspices of what became known as the Nagasaki Flag incident.

Kishi's perceived "anti-Beijing" approach soured Japan's relationship with China (as compared to relations under previous Japanese prime ministers), but the problem was exacerbated by China's hard-line foreign and domestic policies, evidenced in the heightening of tension in the Taiwan Strait, the growing Sino-Soviet schism, and the self-sufficiency policy exemplified in the Great Leap Forward. Trade and exchanges between the two countries suffered until the transition in Japanese leadership in 1960.[82]

### 3.    Ikeda Hayato (1960–1964)

Prime Minister Ikeda visited Yasukuni five times, and each time Beijing looked the other way. The motivations that could account for these outcomes seem to be economic. Following Japan's toxic state of affairs with China under Kishi, Ikeda ushered in a new character of leadership, one that China was receptive to and used to repair the two-year economical drought from the previous prime minister. "Ikeda," according to Chalmers Johnson, "maintained a public hard-line, anti-P.R.C. position to placate the U.S." while supporting various economic initiatives to bring trade with China back to the pre-1957 status quo, which, by 1956, represented nearly thirty percent of Japan's trade in Northeast Asia.[83] The "friendly trade" agreement of 1960 and the Liao-Takasaki trade

[81] Akira Iriye, "Chinese-Japanese Relations, 1945–90," in *The China Quarterly*, no. 124 (1990): 626–27.

[82] Chalmers Johnson, "The Patterns of Japanese Relations with China, 1952–1982," in *Pacific Affairs* 59, no. 3 (1986): 408.

[83] Ibid.; Soeya Yoshihide, *Japan's Economic Diplomacy with China, 1945–1978* (Oxford: Clarendon Press, 1998), 43.

agreement in 1962 serve as two examples of such initiatives.[84]  In this context and with regards to Yasukuni, economic advance trumped unsettled historical scores.

### 4.  Sato Eisaku (1964–1972)

Of all postwar Japanese prime ministers, Prime Minister Sato's eleven visits over eight years were the most by any prime minister to Yasukuni to date, though all eleven visits were done during festivals. China largely ignored all eleven visits.[85]  Yet again, this is not indicative of a healthy relationship between the two countries. Quite to the contrary, the relationship over this period was rather acrimonious. Sato, a member of the Kishi faction of the Liberal Democratic Party, was a vitriolic opponent of Beijing, and Beijing was equally hostile to what was termed the "reactionary Sato government."[86] Similar to Kishi's policies, Sato's pro-Taiwan stance and his proclivity to appease Washington discolored relations with Beijing over this period.

Despite the bilateral tension, however, improvements in China-Japan ties were in the offing. Sato presided over Japan during a period of intense transition with regard to relations with China. Up to 1972, Japan's China policy was constrained by Washington's expectation that Tokyo would follow its lead in isolating the PRC in favor of maintaining ties with ROC. Such constraints frustrated Tokyo's desires to reap the economic benefits of trade with mainland China. Tokyo's creative policy of separating politics from economics (*seikei bunri*) to pursue trade with the PRC circumvented these U.S.-imposed constraints. The shifting geopolitical landscape of the late 1960s and early 1970s,

---

[84] According to Caroline Rose, "Friendly trade, from 1960, involved China's agreement to trade with only those Japanese companies that were deemed to be friendly towards China. Liao-Takasaki trade was named after its architects who signed the Sino-Japanese Long-Term Comprehensive Trade memorandum in 1962 that established semiofficial economic relations between China and Japan where none had existed before and paved the way for future normalization." See notes in Caroline Rose, "Breaking the Deadlock: Japan's informal diplomacy with the People's Republic of China, 1958–9," in *Japanese Diplomacy in the 1950s: From Isolation to Integration*, eds. Iokibe Makoto, et al. (New York: Routledge, 2008), 195, and Itoh Mayumi, *Pioneers of Sino-Japanese Relations* (New York: Palgrave Macmillan, 2012), 1.

[85] On 15 August 1971, Xinhua reported the visit of various Tokyo leaders to the shrine, but not to Sato's actual visits (Sato did not even visit in August 1971). See Peking NCNA International Service in English, August 17, 1971, in FBIS Asia, August 18, 1971, A2.

[86] Numerous *People's Daily* reports during Sato's tenure refer to his regime as "reactionary."  For a detailed account of Beijing's perspective on Sato, see Peking NCNA International Service in English, November 25, 1964, in FBIS *Asia*, November 25, 1964, BBB13–15. Quote from Peking NCNA International Service in English, June 25, 1965, in FBIS Asia, June 28, 1965, BBB8–10.

however, positioned Sato to remedy Japan's informal relationship with China by laying the foundation for a change in the status of relations between Japan and China.

By 1965, Japan had eclipsed the Soviet Union as the PRC's largest trading partner.[87] Economic progress might explain why Beijing chose to ignore Sato's visits to Yasukuni, despite the disharmonious relationship between the two. Sato's next three—visits in 1966, 1967, and 1968—were likely overshadowed by the domestic upheaval in the PRC with the onset of Mao's Great Proletarian Cultural Revolution. What was not overlooked, though, was Sato's September 1967 visit to Chiang Kai-shek in Taipei. Beijing news agencies viciously criticized Sato for being a "faithful running dog of the U.S. imperialists," and for conducting "conspiratorial activities" in Taiwan to build upon a "two China" plot.[88]

Nineteen sixty-nine was a turbulent year in China-Japan relations. Firstly, 1969 marked the centennial of the Yasukuni Shrine. In June, the rightist faction of the LDP introduced a Yasukuni Shrine bill in the Japanese Diet that proposed state sponsorship of the shrine. Beijing was quick to criticize the legislation, stating that the effort revealed Japanese attempts to revive militaristic nationalism.[89] While not in response to either of Sato's spring or autumn visits to the shrine, Beijing's response to the bill indicates that it was aware of Yasukuni and rejected any attempts by Tokyo to support it.

Secondly, Beijing's criticism of Yasukuni was buttressed by increased Japanese Self-Defense Force (SDF) spending, evidenced by Tokyo's purchase of over one hundred F-4 Phantom fighter aircraft and increased defense spending on ground, air, and maritime force structure.[90] The final provocation came in November with the Sato-Nixon

---

[87] Johnson, "The Patterns of Japanese Relations with China, 1952–1982," 406.

[88] Peking NCNA International Service in English, September 10, 1967, in FBIS *Asia*, September 11, 1967, BBB11.

[89] See Peking NCNA International Service in English, July 7, 1969, in FBIS *Asia*, July 7, 1969, A3.

[90] See Peking Domestic Service in Mandarin, December 5, 1969, in FBIS *Asia*, December 11, 1969, A5.

communiqué—a bilateral agreement between Tokyo and Washington that, among several things, called on Japan to take on a greater defense role in the region.[91]

Following the "Nixon shocks" of the summer of 1971, Sato laid the foundation for shifting diplomatic recognition from Taipei to Beijing.[92] In January 1971, despite Beijing's openly hostile polemics towards Tokyo, Sato advised the Diet that normalizing relations with the "People's Republic of China" (the first time he used China's official name) was on the political agenda and started new initiatives to usher in a new China policy.[93] Beijing, however, was so distrustful of Sato that it ignored Sato's request to visit Beijing and delayed diplomatic recognition until Sato was no longer prime minister. Even after Sato relayed his intentions to recognize the PRC as the sole legitimate government of China and of Japan's readiness to abrogate its peace treaty with the ROC, Zhou Enlai eschewed normalization negotiations, stating, "Even if Sato accepted the three basic principles as the basis of opening talks with us, we shall not accept Sato as a negotiating partner."[94] Thus, while normalization initiatives emerged under Sato at the expense of his preferred "two China" policy, the acrimonious relationship China

---

[91] China perceived the communiqué as a step towards a stronger and potentially militaristic Japan, particularly with regard to Japanese security interests being explicitly and inextricably linked to those of Taiwan.

[92] The two Nixon shocks of 1971 refer to the abrupt transformation of the Sino-American relationship and the decision to abandon the Bretton Woods system of international financial exchange. Both shocks represented a dramatic change in the political geometry of the region and presented Tokyo with an opportunity to end the informal economic relationships in favor of full diplomatic recognition. See Miller and Wich, *Becoming Asia*, 175–76.

[93] With regard to Yasukuni, Sato visited the shrine on 22 April 1971, which Beijing ignored. On 15 August, however, the Sato cabinet held World War II commemoration ceremonies in various locations (including one at the Yasukuni Shrine, though not attended by Sato) to which Beijing delivered scathing criticisms. According to Chinese press, August 1971 is the first time Tokyo sponsored such commemorative events. Beijing's reaction demonstrates the lingering sensitivities of Japanese imperialism associated with 15 August, which would have implications for future Japanese administrations. See Peking NCNA International Service in English, August 17, 1971, in FBIS *Asia*, August 18, 1971, A2.

[94] Quoted in Gene Hsiao, "The Sino-Japanese Rapprochement: A Relationship of Ambivalence," in *Sino-American Détente and Its Policy Implications*, ed. Gene Hsiao (New York: Praeger, 1974), 165. The "three principles for the restoration of relations" put forward by the Government of the People's Republic of China in the 1972 Sino-Japanese communiqué, to which Zhou Enlai referred, are "(1) The People's Republic of China is the sole legal government of China; (2) Taiwan is an inalienable part of territory of the People's Republic of China; (3) "Peace Treaty" between Japan and Chiang Kaishek authorities is illegal and it must be abrogated"; quoted from "Bilateral Political Relations," China Internet Information Center, accessed May 2, 2013, http://www.china.org.cn.

maintained with Japan ensured that normalization fell to the next prime minister to conclude.

### 5.    Tanaka Kakuei (1972–1974)

The transition to Prime Minister Tanaka in 1972 allowed the PRC to continue Sato's normalization initiatives while saving face with domestic and international audiences by following through on their policy of not working with regimes unfriendly to China. Tanaka by all accounts was more pragmatic in his economic focus in relations with China compared to Sato, and his previous experience as minister of finance and international trade and industry accounts for his firm belief in the power of money in politics. Chalmers Johnson notes that trade with China continued under Sato but increased dramatically under Tanaka.[95]    Yet, even as economic interests advanced bilateral relations between Japan and China, they also constrained advances toward normalization. Gene Hsiao notes that Japanese trade with Taiwan reached a record high in 1972, and that Japan's close ties with Taiwan impeded Sino-Japanese normalization initiatives. Thus, while the 1972 joint communiqué concluded diplomatic recognition between governments and Sino-Japanese trade substantially increased under Tanaka, unresolved issues—including Taiwan—delayed Tanaka's normalization initiatives (initiated in September 1974) for several years.[96]

During his tenure as prime minister, Tanaka visited the Yasukuni Shrine five times during the spring and autumn festivals, to which Beijing's only objection was over the LDP rightist faction's proposed legislation, not over the visits themselves. The Yasukuni Shrine bill, initiated in 1969, was submitted through both houses of the Diet for six consecutive years, but was ultimately defeated due to overwhelming domestic opposition. Beijing assiduously followed the bill's developments but took no observable action with regards to Tanaka's visits. One possible interpretation of this outcome is that

---

[95] Johnson, "The Patterns of Japanese Relations with China, 1952–1982," 409.

[96] Hsiao, "The Sino-Japanese Rapprochement: A Relationship of Ambivalence," 166–81; Johnson, "The Patterns of Japanese Relations with China, 1952–1982," 413–14. In addition to Taiwan delaying normalization was China's demand for the inclusion of an "anti-hegemony" clause (an unresolved difference from the 1972 Sino-Japanese joint communiqué), to which Tokyo objected for fear of antagonizing Moscow.

while Beijing frowned upon government sponsorship of Yasukuni, Beijing appreciated the economic incentives (such as bilateral agreements on trade and aviation and navigation in 1974, and a fisheries agreement in 1975) that came with cooperation with Japan as opposed to confrontation. Another interpretation is that Japanese prime ministers from Yoshida through Tanaka never visited the shrine in commemoration of the Pacific War—a trend that would soon change.

### 6.    Miki Takeo (1974–1976)

Prime Minister Miki—a noted pro-China politician—visited Yasukuni three times, but, different from his predecessors, Miki's 15 August 1975 visit made him the first prime minister to visit Yasukuni in honor of those Japanese who died in service during the Pacific War. Interestingly, Beijing ignored this visit.

Despite Miki's pro-China stance, relations between the two were strained mainly because of the Taiwan problem. On 5 April 1975, seventeen days before Miki's 22 April 1975 visit to Yasukuni, Chiang Kai-shek died. Miki's public condolences over Chiang's passing discredited him in Beijing's eyes, and the situation was further exacerbated when Miki permitted Sato Eisaku to attend Chiang's funeral in Taiwan. At the same time, Mao's health was failing. One might expect Beijing to seize the opportunity to link Miki's support to Taiwan to his Yasukuni visit, but, yet again, Beijing let it go. Mao's death in September 1976 not only ended a critical period in PRC history, it also might explain why Beijing ignored Miki's visits to Yasukuni.[97]

## B.    DENG ERA YASUKUNI VISITS

In the years following Mao's death in 1976 up to 1989, four Japanese prime ministers visited Yasukuni 27 times. Of the 27 visits, Beijing ignored 23 of them (85 percent), responding only four times (two of which were very minimal responses) and not consecutively (demonstrating inconsistent behavior). These inconsistencies indicate that there is room for interpretation as to why Beijing ignored some visits while protesting others. Moreover, the evidence of increasing responses to a historically

---

[97] Johnson, "The Patterns of Japanese Relations with China, 1952–1982," 415.

significant event where there was none before suggests a shift from Mao's historical narrative depicting China as a powerful, victorious nation unencumbered by past humiliation to one of victimization and confronting China's painful past. By abandoning the once popular victor narrative under Mao in favor of a victimization narrative, the same Japanese provocations once tolerated became events that became increasingly harder for Beijing to ignore.

### 1. Fukuda Takeo (1976–1978)

Prime Minister Fukuda's four visits to Yasukuni included one visit on the sensitive World War II anniversary, yet Beijing did not object to this or the other seasonal visits. The stalled normalization negotiations seemed to eclipse the Yasukuni debate. Coming out of the unfavorable state of Sino-Japanese relations under Miki, Fukuda sought a breakthrough in the normalization deadlock. Trade proved to be the tool of choice for Fukuda.

On 16 February 1978, China and Japan concluded a Long-term (LT) Trade Agreement whereby both sides agreed to $20 billion in trade over eight years.[98] Under the agreement China's energy exports would grow and Japan would export equipment technology needed for Chinese industrialization.[99] The LT trade agreement represented the type of economic enhancement initiatives Beijing both wanted and needed to implement its sought-after reforms.

The highlight of Fukuda's tenure as Japanese prime minister in Sino-Japanese relations was the conclusion of a peace treaty with the PRC that ended the state of war and normalized relations between the two countries. The Chinese proved to be shrewd negotiators, and the treaty reflected that reality by hooking Tokyo into the anti-hegemony clause (an implicit reference to Soviet expansion). In so doing, Tokyo lost all leverage

---

[98] Peking NCNA in English, February 16, 1978, in FBIS *Asia*, February 16, 1978, A5.

[99] The showcase project of the LT trade agreement was the Baoshan steel mill near Shanghai—a massive steel plant with an annual capacity of six million tons. Baoshan was agreed to in principle in 1978, but the Chinese waivered on its funding for several years leading to the 1981 Baoshan Shock whereby Beijing unilaterally cancelled the project (discussed in greater detail in later sections of this chapter). See Allen Whiting, *China Eyes Japan* (Berkeley: University of California Press, 1989), 96–97 and Johnson, "The Patterns of Japanese Relations with China, 1952–1982," 418–19.

with Moscow in negotiating the return of the disputed Northern Territories.[100]  Fukuda, in an unsuccessful attempt to salvage relations with Moscow, demanded China agree to an article stating that the treaty would not constrain either party's relations with third countries. China agreed, but the result was a lopsided treaty that favored China more than it did Japan.

While the treaty represented a landmark advance in Sino-Japanese relationships (certainly an event of the magnitude that could obfuscate Fukuda's visits to Yasukuni), history reveals a slight blemish on what was otherwise a successful and mutually beneficial treaty. On 17 October 1978— one day before the treaty was ratified—fourteen Class A war criminals were interred at Yasukuni.[101]  Though it is unlikely that Beijing knew of the war criminals' interment as it happened (Japanese media made the war criminals' enshrinement public knowledge in 1979), the event would be a dramatic turning point in the Yasukuni controversy years later, putting Beijing in a difficult position where ignoring visits would become increasingly more difficult.

### 2.    Ohira Masayoshi (1978–1980)

Prime Minister Ohira paid three uneventful visits to Yasukuni during seasonal festivals. The first of which occurred in April 1979 during Deng Xiaoping's consolidation of power from Hua Guafeng as China's paramount leader. Perhaps more notable, however, is the Chinese security context in which this visit occurred. Two months earlier China was at war with Vietnam. The brief conflict lasted less than three weeks and demonstrated a lackluster performance on the part of the PLA, particularly

---

[100] Moscow was not a signatory to the San Francisco treaty and as such remained in a state of conflict with Japan until the signing of the Joint Declaration of 1956, which, while short of a formal peace treaty, ended the state of war and established diplomatic relations between the two. At issue was the larger issue of a peace treaty and the sovereignty of the four southernmost Kuril Islands, or Northern Territories in Japan. As part of the joint declaration, Japan and the Soviet Union agreed to continue negotiations to conclude a formal peace treaty and normalize relations, and, upon a formal peace, the Soviet Union would also turn over the islands of Habomai and Shikotan to Japan. The negotiations failed, however, for reasons inclusive of the Sino-Japanese peace treaty and the presence of U.S. forces in Japan, and both the peace treaty and the territorial dispute remain unresolved today. See Miller and Wich, *Becoming Asia*, 60, and the Japanese Ministry of Foreign Affairs, "Joint Compendium of Documents on the History of Territorial Issue between Japan and Russia," last accessed May 14, 2013,
http://www.mofa.go.jp/region/europe/russia/territory/edition92/preface.html .

[101] Phil Deans, "Diminishing Returns? Prime Minister Koizumi's Visits to the Yasukuni Shrine in the Context of East Asian Nationalisms." *East Asia* 24 (2007): 282.

with regard to shortcomings in combined arms operations and command and control. To rectify this security gap, and the economy more broadly, Deng moved to advance the "four modernizations" initiative by soliciting help from Japan.[102] Additionally, Deng requested Japanese low-interest loans and cooperation on developing China's legal system to help manage the inflow of foreign capital funding these modernizations.[103] With such modernization progress riding on Japanese assistance, one can reasonably conclude that Beijing had ample incentive not to upset the status of Sino-Japanese relations over Yasukuni.

### 3. Suzuki Zenko (1980–1982)

Since becoming prime minister after Ohira's sudden death, Suzuki Zenko visited Yasukuni nine times in just over two years—the most aggressive pattern at that time since 1951 with visits every spring, autumn, and August. No observable response from Beijing could be found for the first seven visits, which, when taken into account the two 15 August visits, suggest that Beijing continued to have economic motivations to ignore the visits, such as the cooperative joint Baoshan steel mill venture. Japan would soon realize the risk of such joint ventures.

In 1981, after years of construction and Japanese aid, Beijing unilaterally cancelled Baoshan steel mill contracts with Japan, worth ¥300 billion. The motivations for Beijing's actions are not entirely clear, although some argue the decision was driven by Chinese fiscal constraints and bureaucratic dissatisfaction with the project.[104] The "Baoshan shock" created an air of uncertainty in Japan about the prospects of trade with China, and even threatened the future of the LT trade agreement. To salvage investment, Japan provided China an additional ¥300 billion for Baoshan to resume. The implications

---

[102] The four modernizations, adopted at the Third Plenum of the 11th Central Committee of the CCP in 1978, focused on agriculture, industry, science and technology, and national defense, and formed the foundation of Chinese reforms that continue to this day. See Dennis Blasko, *The Chinese Army Today* (New York: Routledge, 2012), 4.

[103] *Kyodo* in English, May 31, 1979, in FBIS *Asia*, June 1, 1979, D6; *Kyodo* in English, June 19, 1979, in FBIS *Asia*, June 20, 1979, D2.

[104] See Whiting, *China Eyes Japan*, 96–97 and Johnson, "The Patterns of Japanese Relations with China, 1952–1982," 418–19.

of Baoshan, and Sino-Japanese economic integration more broadly, indicate that the health of the economy was more important than historic controversy.

The history issue took a turn on 26 June 1982 when Japanese media reported that the Japanese government had ordered revision of Japanese history textbooks in ways that diminished early 20th century Japanese Imperial Army conduct.[105] The headlines drew quick condemnation from Beijing and Seoul.[106] Chalmers Johnson argues that Beijing was not insulted over the textbook issue as much as it was an effort by Deng to divert attention away from Japan's renewed ties to Taiwan—evidenced by the near simultaneous visit of the LDP's Special Council for International Economic Policy to Taiwan. Twenty days later, on the sensitive date of 15 August, Suzuki visited Yasukuni. Suzuki's Yasukuni visit would seem to have added welcome fuel to the diversionary fires as the visit preceded the twelfth CCP National Party Congress—the event for which Deng would come under fire from Party rivals about being soft on anything having to do with Taiwan. Beijing did respond, however, but minimally. While the *People's Daily* ran a lengthy report on Yasukuni, it did not officially condemn Suzuki's visit; rather, it questioned whether Japan had learned anything from World War II.[107]

Notable, though, was that Xinhua reported that Suzuki had made the visit in an official capacity by signing the visitor's book as "prime minister."[108] The official capacity of this visit is important because it challenges the conventional wisdom that Prime Minister Nakasone Yasuhiro's 1985 visit was the first official visit of a Japanese prime minister to Yasukuni. That there was no international outrage associated with Suzuki's visit and attendant statements suggests that the visits themselves were not the problem and that Beijing manufactured the problem to suit its interests.

Suzuki visited Yasukuni two months later in October. Beijing did not officially object to his visit, but the media seized upon another visit to the shrine to bring awareness

---

[105] Xinhua in English, June 26, 1982, in FBIS *Asia*, July 7, 1982, D2.

[106] For Beijing's response, see *Renmin Ribao* in Chinese, July 20, 1982, in FBIS *Asia*, July 21, 1982, D3.

[107] *Renmin Ribao* in Chinese, August 15, 1982, in FBIS *Asia*, August 18, 1982, D2.

[108] Xinhua in English, August 15, 1982, in FBIS *Asia*, August 17, 1982, D8; Hsin Wan Pao in Chinese, August 16, 1982, in FBIS Asia, August 17, 1982, W4.

to the event. The Xinhua news agency reported that 139 Dietmen visited Yasukuni and that the Suzuki administration had deemed such visits might be in violation of Japan's Constitution.[109]  While this report was minimal and did not even address Suzuki's 18 October 1982 visit, it did demonstrate the increasing awareness of Yasukuni in China, and, because of the timing of the Xinhua report, a link to Suzuki's visit can be inferred, and so counts as an objection.

### 4.        Nakasone Yasuhiro (1982–1987)

By the time Nakasone Yasuhiro succeeded Suzuki as prime minister, Japan had become an economic superpower (the second largest world economy since 1970), and Nakasone sought to raise Japan's geopolitical role commensurate with its status. While such a stance might normally have come at the cost of improved relations with Beijing, Nakasone sought to improve relations with China, and Beijing was receptive.[110]  While Nakasone enhanced bilateral trade, however, he concomitantly stoked the embers of anti-Japanese nationalism in China with his visits to Yasukuni.

Initially Beijing seemed to be on a course to ignore Nakasone's visits. Nakasone's first visit was in April 1983, which occurred against a backdrop of improved Sino-Japanese relations. In an interview with the *People's Daily*, Nakasone stated, "Japan wants to establish firm scientific and cultural exchanges with China on the basis of mutual economic cooperation."[111]  Nakasone's visit in August, however, proved that Yasukuni would be a source of friction between the two states.

Dating back to 1951, Nakasone's 15 August 1983 visit was historic in that it was the first time Beijing, in no ambiguous language, condemned the Japanese prime minister for visiting the Yasukuni Shrine. The *People's Daily* ran several headlines that criticized Nakasone's visit. Beijing objected despite its ongoing $5 billion loan negotiations for the buildup of critical infrastructure, including port expansion and railway construction in

---

[109] Xinhua in English, October 19, 1982, in FBIS *Asia*, October 21, 1982, D2.

[110] Miller and Wich, *Becoming Asia,* 195.

[111] Kyodo in English, January 6, 1983, in FBIS *Asia*, January 6, 1983, C1.

northern China and joint offshore oil exploration in the Bohai Sea.[112] Loan negotiations carried through the next several years, which may have had in impact on Beijing's decision to ignore Nakasone's following seven visits to Yasukuni (October 1983 - April 1985). The event suggests that the Yasukuni problem had evolved since the Mao years, because this marks the first time Beijing was willing to raise the history issue at the potential expense of considerable loans.

Interestingly, on 10 August 1984 and ahead of his upcoming 15 August visit to Yasukuni, Nakasone commented to Japanese media, "I [Nakasone] will visit the Shrine [Yasukuni] on 15 August to commemorate the end of World War II. I will make the visit as 'Prime Minister Yasuhiro Nakasone' as before."[113] Following the visit, Xinhua reported on Nakasone's visit and pointed out that Nakasone offered a ¥100,000 donation "in his capacity as prime minister."[114] Similar to Suzuki's August 1982 visit, Nakasone explicitly stated that he made his visits to the shrine in an official capacity; yet no international outrage emerged in this instance.

Nakasone's last visit to the Yasukuni Shrine was on 15 August 1985—the 40th anniversary of the end of World War II. A day before the visit, the PRC Ministry of Foreign Affairs (MOFA) cautioned Tokyo that Nakasone's visit would "hurt the feelings of the Chinese."[115] The warnings went unheeded, and after Nakasone's visit thousands of Chinese students staged anti-Japanese protests in Beijing and Xian. The protests went on for days and seemed to have the regime's support. Politburo member Hu Qili commented that the protests were "understandable," and that he "did all kinds of (similar) things when [he] was young."[116] The visceral response in Beijing—criticisms from Deng Xiaoping, MOFA, the media, the CPPCC, and three days of student protests—convinced Nakasone not visit the shrine again.

---

112 Kyodo in English, February 19, 1983, in FBIS *Asia*, February 23, 1983, D1; Xinhua in English, September 3, 1983, in FBIS *Asia*, September 9, 1983, D3.

113 Yomiuri Shimbun in Japanese, August 11, 1984, in FBIS *Asia*, August 14, 1984, 5.

114 Xinhua in English, August 15, 1984, in FBIS *Asia*, August 16, 1984, D2.

115 Xinhua in English, August 14, 1985, in FBIS *Asia*, August 14, 1985, A1.

116 Hong Kong AFP in English, October 3, 1985, in FBIS *Asia*, October 4, 1985, D1.

Notable is the Chinese domestic and political context in which Nakasone's visit occurred. In 1985, Japan was running an estimated $1 billion in trade surplus with China.[117] The Chinese populace, insulted by Nakasone's visit and perceived economic exploitation of a weaker country, charged that reliance on Japanese investment to fund China's economic modernizations was akin to a Japanese "second invasion."[118] Hu Yaobang, then-CCP general secretary and advocate of friendly relations with Japan, used a soft domestic approach to the demonstrations, mixing minimum force and maximum persuasion to end the demonstrations, so as to avoid disruption to ongoing economic initiatives, such as Baoshan.[119] In the international forum, Chinese Foreign Minister Wu Xueqian admonished Japan "not to go back to the old militarist road," in an effort to appease Chinese audiences.[120]

Protests continued through December 1985 before they were eventually squelched, but a door had been opened that the regime could not fully close. The PRC's repression of anti-Japanese demonstrations led to a recurrence a year later, only in 1986 the larger demonstrations focused more on China's own political system than on Japan. Infuriated by the demonstrations, Deng ousted Hu from power, which in-turn had linkages to the 1989 student protests in Beijing.[121] The 1985 visit and its resultant political repression earned Hu Yaobang the label of "pro-Japan faction" and set the precedent for future generations of Chinese leaders against taking a soft approach towards Japan.[122]

---

[117] Kyodo in English, December 7, 1985, in Joint Publications Research Service *China Report*, January 8, 1986, 8.

[118] Quoted in Whiting, *China Eyes Japan*, 67.

[119] On the PRC's political repression in response to the demonstrations, Allen Whiting states, "The regime reacted with lengthy articles, meetings with students, and high-level diplomacy." See Whiting, *China Eyes Japan*, 67, 70.

[120] Hsin Wan Pao in Chinese, October 13, 1985, in FBIS *Asia*, October 18, 1985.

[121] The student demonstrations provided the proximate cause of Hu's ousting, but the long term cause was Hu's perceived application of "bourgeois liberalization," or "negating the socialist system in favor of the capitalist system," which ultimately conflicted with Deng's four cardinal principles of adherence to Party leadership, to Mao Zedong thought, to the people's democratic dictatorship, and to the socialist road. Quoted from *Renmin Ribao* in Chinese, January 1, 1987, in FBIS Asia, January 5, 1987, K6.

[122] Whiting, *China Eyes Japan*, 66–79; Susan Shirk, *China: Fragile Superpower* (New York: Oxford University Press, 2008), 160–64.

The extreme response from China to Nakasone's 1985 visit likely received the attention it did because it coincided with the 40th anniversary of World War II—not from the official capacity of the visit, as other visits were clearly done in the same capacity. Additionally, the Class A war criminals added intensity to the complaint, rather than the basis for it. In response, Nakasone cancelled his planned autumn visit to Yasukuni, and any future visits as well. The next visit occurred eleven years later.

## C.    POST-TIANANMEN YASUKUNI VISITS

The Tiananmen massacre fundamentally altered the state-society social contract in China, and the ghosts of Tiananmen still haunt the regime by constraining Beijing's foreign policy options whenever Japanese provocations arise. Japanese provocations hold significant potential to generate swells of anti-Japanese nationalism that can result in Chinese domestic unrest. Beijing, embracing this reality, controls the media and security forces in attempts to suppress public opinion in some cases and to mobilize it in others. Beijing's 100 percent response pattern to Japanese prime minister visits to Yasukuni in the years following 1989 attests to this reality. Moreover, Chinese leaders in the 1990s and after have commanded less presence than the cult of personality of Chairman Mao or the paramount stature of Deng Xiaoping. Thus, one way to consolidate power is to reinvigorate history issues and generate popular animosity towards Japan.

### 1.    Hashimoto Ryotaro (1996–1998)

Prime Minister Hashimoto visited Yasukuni but one time in the summer of 1996 on his birthday. While his visit was in July, one might conclude that the visit was divorced from the tension that August visits generate.[123] Beijing, however, drew no such distinction. The *People's Daily* wrote a scathing critique of Hashimoto and Japanese

---

[123] In Japanese domestic politics, 1993 was a landmark year when the Democratic Party of Japan (DPJ) defeated the LDP in national elections. The DPJ did not retain power for long. In 1996, the Hashimoto-led LDP reasserted its claim over Japanese politics. In this context, Hashimoto's visit to Yasukuni could be interpreted as political maneuvering to appeal to domestic audiences and garner conservative voter support in the upcoming Japanese general elections.

leaders who visited the shrine.[124]  Beijing's response came on the heels of what was already a turbulent moment in the security picture of Northeast Asia: The March 1996 Taiwan Straits crisis, the April 1996 U.S.-Japan Joint Declaration on Security, and the July 1996 territorial dispute over the uninhabited islets in the East China Sea, known as Senkaku in Japanese and Diaoyu in Chinese.[125]

Hashimoto did not return to Yasukuni for the remainder of his term. For its part, the Beijing regime probably concluded that it had successfully pressured Hashimoto the same way it had done in 1985 with Nakasone. It would soon find out that pressure does not work on everyone.

## 2.    Koizumi Junichiro (2001–2006)

Prime Minister Koizumi represented a new generation of revisionists in Japanese politics whose anti-China attitude was very popular amongst domestic audiences but quite unpopular with Chinese. A persistent source of friction between Koizumi and Beijing since before Koizumi was even elected was the issue of Yasukuni. Koizumi visited Yasukuni six times—once every year of his term. Beijing responded to each visit with official objections.

In Beijing during 2001, the leadership had yet to transition from Jiang Zemin to Hu Jintao. Jiang, remembering the ghosts of Tiananmen, was keenly attuned to the power of nationalist public opinion and made efforts to mobilize that opinion against Japan. In contrast, Hu, not bringing the same anti-Japanese emotional baggage into the presidency, made cautious efforts to smooth over differences with Koizumi to harmonize bilateral relations while ensuring domestic stability.[126]  Koizumi was less accommodating. As mentioned in Chapter One, Beijing's efforts to negotiate a less contentious visit to Yasukuni in 2001 failed, leaving few options but to lodge official protest in the

---

[124] As reported in Xinhua in English, August 16, 1996, Open Source Center, accessed May 6, 2013, https://www.opensource.gov/portal/server.pt/gateway/PTARGS_0_0_200_0_0_43/content/Display/505389

[125] Sasajima, Masahiko, "Japan's Domestic Politics and China Policymaking," in *An Alliance for Engagement: Building Cooperation in Security Relations with China*, eds. Benjamin Self and Jeffrey Thompson (Washington, DC: The Henry L. Stimson Center, 2002), 84.

[126] Shirk, *China: Fragile Superpower*, 164, 177.

aftermath.[127] Similar to 1996, the response was high on rhetoric but low on action. Beijing likely thought that by levying pressure in the same manner that it did during the tenure of Hashimoto and Nakasone, it could coerce Koizumi to refrain from future visits. Koizumi's return to Yasukuni in April 2002, however, demonstrated that he was not going to be persuaded as his predecessors had been. Beijing again lodged an official protest in 2002, including a statement from the Foreign Ministry that the visit was "a mistake" and that it "damaged the political foundation of Sino-Japanese ties."[128]

Koizumi's surprise visit in January 2003 invited similar heated polemics. Beijing was particularly critical of what it perceived as an attempt by Koizumi to avoid international observance by visiting in January.[129] Despite Beijing's condemnation of the visit, bilateral economic and diplomatic initiatives continued through the year, including two summits between Koizumi and Hu Jintao.[130]

In 2004, Koizumi again visited in January, and again Beijing responded with an official protest. But this visit occurred during a downturn in bilateral relations, and it appeared to mark a shift in Chinese society's acceptance of Beijing's handling of the provocations. In August 2003, an unearthed Japanese chemical munition exploded in Qiqihar city, wounding 37.[131] Then, in September, a sex scandal in Zuhai involving hundreds of Japanese businessmen and Chinese prostitutes stoked Chinese nationalist

---

[127] See *Renmin Ribao* in Chinese, August 14, 2001, Open Source Center, accessed May 6, 2013, https://www.opensource.gov/portal/server.pt/gateway/PTARGS_0_0_200_203_121123_43/content/Display /CPP20010814000045#.

[128] In 2002, the response was high in rhetoric but also higher in response as compared to 2001. Sasajima Masahiko points out that China postponed a visiting Japanese delegation from the Ministry of State for Defense and also the visit of Chinese naval vessels to Japan. For Beijing's response, see Beijing Ministry of Foreign Affairs of the People's Republic of China in Chinese, April 23, 2002, Open Source Center, accessed May 6, 2013, https://www.opensource.gov/portal/server.pt/gateway/PTARGS_0_0_200_203_121123_43/content/Display /CPP20020423000113#. Also see Sasajima, Masahiko, "Japan's Domestic Politics and China Policymaking," in *An Alliance for Engagement: Building Cooperation in Security Relations with China*, eds. Benjamin Self and Jeffrey Thompson (Washington, DC: The Henry L. Stimson Center, 2002), 82.

[129] *Renmin Ribao* in Chinese, January 15, 2003, Open Source Center, accessed May 14, 2013, https://www.opensource.gov/portal/server.pt/gateway/PTARGS_0_0_200_203_121123_43/content/Display /CPP20030115000045#.

[130] See Ed Griffith, "The Three Phases of China's Response to Koizumi and the Yasukuni Shrine Issue: Structuration in Sino-Japanese Relations," *European Research Center on Contemporary Taiwan Online Paper Series* (2012), 17.

[131] James Reilly, *Strong Society, Smart State* (New York: Columbia University Press, 2012), 140.

embers when the media reported that the event occurred on the eve of the 72nd anniversary of Japan's invasion of Manchuria in 1931.[132] Taken together, all three events represent a steady deterioration in bilateral ties, which came to a boiling point the following year.

Though Koizumi's 2005 visit happened in October, the highpoint in tensions was months earlier in April, when anti-Japanese protests rocked Beijing and Shanghai. The proximate cause of the riots was Japan's bid for permanent membership to the United Nations Security Council, but the tension had been steadily building, attributable to several factors, not least of which Koizumi's continued visits to Yasukuni. The demonstrations went on for weeks before the regime stepped in and put a stop to them.[133] Months later, in October, Koizumi paid tribute at Yasukuni, to which the PRC Foreign Ministry stated, "The Chinese Government resolutely opposes Prime Minister Koizumi's visit to Yasukuni Shrine."[134]

Koizumi's last visit to the shrine was on 15 August 2006. Aware of his short time left in office, Koizumi felt no compunction about visiting on such a highly sensitive date, leaving any political fallout for his replacement to handle. President Hu Jintao lambasted Koizumi for this visit, along with the previous five, but more importantly, Hu used the occasion to sensitize the incoming Japanese leadership of the importance that China attaches to the Yasukuni problem and that improved bilateral ties were dependent upon Japan ceasing the visits. As of this writing, Koizumi was the last prime minister to visit Yasukuni.

---

[132] James Przystup, "Japan-China Relations: Cross Currents," Institute for National and Strategic Studies, The National Defense University, accessed May 6, 2013, http://csis.org/files/media/csis/pubs/0304qjapan_china.pdf.

[133] The regime attempted to control the wave of anti-Japanese nationalism by imposing media blackouts to hinder organization efforts and used Beijing police and the People's Armed Police to monitor the demonstrations as they occurred. See Shirk, *China: Fragile Superpower*, 141–43.

[134] Xinhua in Chinese, October 20, 2005, Open Source Center, accessed May 6, 2013, https://www.opensource.gov/portal/server.pt/gateway/PTARGS_0_0_200_0_0_43/content/Display/567615 8.

# D.    ANALYSIS OF BEIJING'S RESPONSES

## 1.    Beijing's Responses by the Numbers

Of the 64 Japanese prime minister visits to Yasukuni, Beijing responded 11 times (17 percent) while ignoring the majority, 53 (83 percent). Broken down by the different periods used in this thesis, Mao ignored all thirty visits, Deng ignored 23 visits and responded four times, and the post-1989 leadership responded to each of the seven visits. Of the 11 responses, five were in response to visits during the sensitive month of August, which was the clear majority over any other month of the year (two in October, two in January, and one in April and July). Thus, if Beijing was going to react, the majority of the time it did so in response to August visits.

## 2.    Chinese Trends and Explanations

From the preceding analysis, two periods of consistency emerge. First, Mao ignored every visit. Second, the post-1989 leaders responded to every visit. Deng Xiaoping represents the only era when Beijing was inconsistent in response to Yasukuni. Such a trend lends much credibility to the assertion that Mao, the founding dictator of the People's Republic, had unchallenged authority on matters of foreign policy. After Mao, a trend suggestive of a lessening of the authority that Mao commanded emerges, evidenced in this case by several instances of government responses to Yasukuni under Deng and 100 percent under leaders thereafter.

The lingering question is what explains Beijing's responses to Yasukuni? Scholarship cites two reasons that account for the reversal in Beijing's approach to Yasukuni: either the inclusion of Class A war criminals or the official capacity of the visits. While these factors are important, perhaps the best explanation is one that does not stress either reason, but parses together changing domestic conditions in China with the evolution of changes in the Yasukuni problem.

One interpretation of Beijing's reversal from ignoring Yasukuni Shrine visits from 1950 to 1984 to actively protesting prime minister visits in 1985 focuses on the enshrinement of Class A war criminals and the symbol such visits represent toward honoring Japan's imperialistic past. In this context, prior to 1978 Beijing largely ignored shrine visits presumably because the visits did not present a serious agitation to Chinese historical memory by honoring those convicted of the most egregious war crimes. Given that neither Chinese political elites nor popular levels of Chinese society seemed to object when Class B and C war criminals were interred in 1959, one might conclude that the deification of 14 Class A war criminals—seven of which were executed while in Sugamo Prison—was the defining explanation for the fervent government protest witnessed in 1985. Such an explanation, however, is less than compelling given that in April 1979 the media revealed the surreptitious interment of the Class A war criminals.[135] Following April 1979 there were twenty-one prime minister visits to the Yasukuni Shrine that went by relatively unnoticed. If Beijing's staunch protest of Yasukuni was because of the Class A war criminals, then why did Beijing silently endure over twenty prime minister visits to the shrine?

Another explanation suggests that the vehement response in 1985 was not because of the enshrinement of 14 Class A war criminals, but rather because Prime Minister Nakasone Yasuhiro declared his visit in August 1985 to be official. During his visit, Nakasone included his title as prime minister in signing the Yasukuni guest book and paid for both the entrance fee and a wreath with state funds. In this context, Nakasone increased the level of provocation by linking the state of Japan to honoring war criminals in a way not previously seen. Beijing reacted to this subtle revisionist gesture rather than the visit itself. However, this explanation also falls short, given that Nakasone had visited the shrine nine times prior to August 1985 largely without incident and ignores Suzuki's previous official visits.

The most compelling explanation for why Beijing reacted in August 1985 in a way previously unseen takes a more systemic analysis inclusive of both arguments but also takes inventory of the changing political landscape of China. The changing of state leadership from Mao to Deng ushered in a new era of authoritarian rule, as previously outlined. Concurrently, the Yasukuni problem evolved into something more complex than it had been in previous decades, with the enshrinement of war criminals and

---

[135] Takenaka, Akiko, "Enshrinement Politics: War Dead and War Criminals at Yasukuni Shrine," *The Asia-Pacific Journal: Japan Focus*, accessed May 15, 2013, http://www.japanfocus.org.

attention to the character of the visits themselves. Taken together, these three factors provide a compelling explanation for Beijing's changing response to Yasukuni.

## E.  CONCLUDING REMARKS

Using Yasukuni Shrine as a test case, the evidence of Beijing's response seems to support Gries's argument that Mao suppressed historical memory of Japanese imperialism to construct a new narrative of a powerful China rather than dwelling on its humiliating past. The combination of Mao's death and the controversial enshrinement of Class A war criminals at Yasukuni contributed towards the shift away from suppression of public opinion regarding historical scores. Based on the Yasukuni trends, one might deduce a link between power and anti-Japanese rhetoric: The more powerful the regime's central figure, the less likely the need to mobilize nationalistic sentiment. Though never formally holding the title of Party general secretary or state president, Deng was China's paramount leader, and held considerable power over the Party and politics. His soft touch on foreign policy issues probably contributed towards improved China-Japan relations than existed under his protégés. Jiang Zemin, on the other hand, appeared weaker and struggled to consolidate power, oftentimes mobilizing anti-Japan nationalism to replace what he lacked in veteran revolutionary bona fides. Hu Jintao was not even considered China's "core leader" as Jiang was and bilateral relations were terrible (to be fair, Prime Minister Koizumi was more provocative than his Japanese predecessors). The increasing responses to Yasukuni suggest that China's post- Mao and Deng leaders may have a greater need to mobilize public sentiment against Japan.

Beyond state leadership, China's political system mattered in how the response to Yasukuni was administered. During the Mao years, political suppression of anti-Japanese nationalism was normal. The authoritarian setting under Mao was one of obedience to Party ideology. Regarding Japan, establishing and normalizing relations was the task at hand, so much so that war reparations were not even demanded. Under Deng, strengthening bilateral ties with Japan for economic benefits was the priority. The anti-Japanese protests witnessed in 1985 seemed to be bottom-up social movements that challenged Party economic initiatives, and were thus suppressed. The inconsistencies with Beijing's responses during this period could have been a reflection of Deng's broader policy volatility. The strong responses seen in 1996 and from 2001–2006 seemed to originate at the top, evidenced by the 2005 anti-Japanese demonstrations.

Beijing's responses to Yasukuni reveal much about authoritarian political systems: The government has greater latitude to respond or ignore public opinion in ways that would challenge a democracy. The South Korean case study affords observers the chance to see how a government responds to Yasukuni in under both authoritarian and democratizing banners.

# V. SEOUL'S RESPONSE TO JAPANESE PRIME MINISTER VISITS TO YASUKUNI

The ROK offers a useful case study for this thesis as it provides a view into Seoul's responses to Japanese prime minister visits to Yasukuni in both an authoritarian and a (transitional) democratic setting. This chapter measures Seoul's public response to each of the 64 prime ministerial visits to Yasukuni and determines what patterns exist and why. Using the periods of ROK authoritarianism and transitional democracy, the study follows a chronology of Japan's prime ministers to assess Seoul's response to their visits to Yasukuni.

Similar to Beijing, Seoul has both ignored Yasukuni visits and has lodged official objection to them. A key difference in the South Korean case study is that there were no periods of inconsistency in the responses. This chapter shows that prior to 1996, Seoul ignored all 57 visits, which encompassed the entirety of the ROK's authoritarian governance. In 1996, Seoul reversed this pattern and began to voice its objection to Tokyo, and has consistently done so henceforth.

## A. AUTHORITARIAN SOUTH KOREAN GOVERNMENT RESPONSES TO YASUKUNI

Between 1951 and 1985, Japanese prime ministers visited the Yasukuni Shrine 57 times. Seoul ignored all 57 visits. Absent any observable response or published policy with which to demonstrate Seoul's position on the matter, one must look to the status of ROK-Japan relations to explain what might account for this pattern. The period of authoritarianism in the ROK spanned its beginnings as a sovereign state in 1948 to 1988. Seoul's politics over this period were dominated by three figures: Rhee Syngman, Park Chung-hee, and Chun Doo-hwan. As Korea's economy reached takeoff in the late 1970s, it looked to Japan as a model of economic success worthy of emulation. In this context, one might interpret Seoul's response to Yasukuni as a conscious decision to focus on building its economy rather than settling historical grievances with Japan. Another plausible explanation might lie in the character, authority, and vision of the successive heads of state in regard to the need to mobilize anti-Japanese nationalism in pursuit of national interests. The following analysis explores these interpretations and concludes that both have explanatory value.

### 1.     Yoshida Shigeru (1948–1954)

At roughly the same time Prime Minister Yoshida was elected to his post, Rhee Syngman took control of the ROK. Seoul ignored Yoshida's five Yasukuni visits, but one must consider the ROK's domestic security context during which these visits occurred. Rhee presided over a country engaged in a brutal civil war and likely had little interest in protesting Yoshida's Yasukuni visits in 1951, 1952, and April 1953. Yoshida's visit in October 1953 was but months after the signing of the armistice agreement on 27 July 1953. Not only was the security situation still very tenuous in the ROK, the country was broken from war.

As the ROK moved on from the war, Rhee remained extremely distrustful of Japan and, as a result, adopted a hostile posture in his relations with Tokyo. Bilateral economic or political engagement can be characterized as minimal, consisting primarily of negotiations on the nationality and status of Koreans in Japan. Trade with Japan existed, consisting mostly of Japanese imports, but was relatively low compared to trade with the United States.[136]   Rhee's non-responses to Yoshida's visits to Yasukuni, however, seem driven less by economic enhancement opportunities, and more reflective of a choice to engage Japan on as little as possible.

### 2.     Kishi Nobusuke (1957–1960)

In 1957, the ROK was importing nearly three times as much from Japan as it was exporting to Japan, likely because the ROK did not have much to export at the time.[137] The imbalance in imports to exports observed in 1957 laid the foundation of the ROK's trade deficit with its neighbor.

---

[136] Bank of Korea 1956 estimates list overall South Korean trade with the United States at $98 million and $29 million with Japan. See Lee Chong-sik, *Japan and Korea: The Political Dimension* (Stanford: Hoover Institution Press, 1985), 88.

[137] According to the Bank of Korea, in 1957 South Korea exported $11 million to Japan and imported $34 million from it. See Lee, *Japan and Korea*, 88.

Seoul ignored both of Prime Minister Kishi's visits to Yasukuni, and, similar to Rhee's relations with Japan under Yoshida, the decision was unlikely tied to trade. In April 1957, shortly after Kishi took office, there was a brief period during which tension in the bilateral relationship subsided. Rhee was willing to reopen the Japanese-Korean talks with Kishi (ahead of Kishi's June visit to the United States) so long as Japan "does not change its sincere attitude."[138] The talks were scuttled, however, based on Seoul's perception that Kishi negotiated $5 billion in loans from Washington for an Asian economic development fund that would expand Japanese trade in Southeast Asia.[139]

By 1960, South Korean trade with Japan had increased to $91 million, nearly doubling 1957 levels.[140] While economic cooperation existed, it is hard to conclude that Rhee's decision to ignore Kishi's Yasukuni visits was premised upon it. A more compelling interpretation is that Rhee desired as little contact as possible, even if it involved ignoring a historical slight.

### 3.    Ikeda Hayato (1960–1964)

Four of Ikeda's five visits to Yasukuni occurred during the turbulent Korean political transition between Rhee's resignation in 1960 and Park Chung-hee's consolidation of power in 1962. One could conclude that the Yasukuni issue was lost in the political turmoil. The first visit that Park could have presumably challenged was Ikeda's 1963 visit. Park's determination to mend relations with Japan early in his tenure, however, suggests that he would have ignored the Yasukuni controversy.

### 4.    Sato Eisaku (1964–1972)

Park's incentive to ignore Yasukuni continued into Prime Minister Sato's term. All eleven of Sato's visits were ignored, but important to note is the context that normalization of relations had on South Korean public opinion.

---

138 Seoul in Japanese to Japan, April 9, 1957, in FBIS *Asia*, April 10, 1957, KKK1.

139 The 1957 joint communiqué between Kishi Nobusuke and Dwight Eisenhower stressed the importance of free Asian nations building strong economies to resist Communist penetration; however, no evidence could be found to support Seoul's claim that Kishi's request for U.S. financial resources was realized. See Seoul in Japanese to Japan, July 11, 1957, in FBIS *Asia*, July 12, 1957, KKK1.

140 Lee, *Japan and Korea,* 88.

Japan and the ROK concluded diplomatic recognition and normalization on 22 June 1965. While normalization was a crucial component of Park's vision for South Korea's economic future, the Korean populace reacted harshly at what it perceived as being betrayed by its own government. The ensuing Korean demonstrations and resultant forceful response set the precedent for state-society relations. In so doing, Park made it clear that there were limits to public dissent, and exceeding those limits could result in forceful response. Park's brutal suppression also demonstrated the importance he attached to the ROK's relations with Japan. In this context, it is reasonable to conclude that even if South Korean society was aware of Sato's subsequent ten visits to Yasukuni, Park's violent political suppression in 1965 ensured that public opinion did not guide policy nor challenge the regime.

The economic benefits of Park's decision to normalize relations with Japan were quickly realized. In 1966, Japan eclipsed the United States as the ROK's largest trading partner.[141] The Yasukuni problem was likely dismissed not only because of the domestic unrest it might generate within the ROK, but mobilizing public opinion against Japan could have also jeopardized the economic cooperation the ROK enjoyed with Japan. The amicable relationship between the two countries, however, was about to change.

## 5.    Tanaka Kakuei (1972–1974)

In 1973 and 1974, two events strained bilateral ties nearly to the breaking point: (1) the 1973 kidnapping of Kim Dae-jung from a Tokyo hotel, and (2) the 1974 assassination attempt of President Park by a Korean resident of Japan.[142] But changes in the ROK's political winds and the effects of the recalibrating Cold War strategic realignment in the early 1970s shaped Korea's domestic environment that set the stage for contention years before either event occurred.

Under the South Korean Constitution at the time, there were term limits on the presidency, which drove the need for elections (despite their perfunctory nature). The

---

[141] In 1966, South Korean trade with Japan equaled $360 million, while that with the United States equaled $349 million. See Lee, *Japan and Korea,* 88.

[142] Ibid., 81.

outcome of the 1971 South Korean national elections, however, was unexpected and shocked the regime. While Park defeated opposition leader Kim Dae-jung, he did so only by a narrow margin (9 percent). Park's near defeat at the elections caused him to take inventory of his political power, and he began to explore ways to strengthen the presidency.

Contemporaneously, the tectonic shifts in the geopolitical landscape produced by the Nixon doctrine and Nixon shocks caused Park to question the commitment of the United States to the defense of South Korea. In a move to hedge against abandonment by the United States, Park hastily established a dialogue with North Korea, and in May 1972, Seoul and Pyongyang leaders met in Pyongyang and agreed on the principles of reunification.[143] The agreement failed to produce any real improvement in South Korea's security, which, when combined with rising political opposition, caused Park to declare a state of martial law in October 1972.[144]

In November, Park drafted a new constitution (known as the Yushin Constitution) that, according to Bruce Cummings, granted him unlimited tenure in office and gave him "powers to appoint and dismiss the cabinet and even the prime minister, to designate one-third of the National Assembly, to suspend or destroy civil liberties, and to issue decrees for whatever powers the Yushin framers forgot to include."[145] Upon hearing of Seoul's dramatic authoritarian thrust, Kim Dae-jung (who by this time had fled to Japan to avoid imprisonment) denounced Park's actions and attempted to rally support against him.[146]

On 8 August 1973, Kim was kidnapped from his hotel room in Tokyo and was held for five days before being released near his home in Seoul.[147] Kim's kidnapping caused an international uproar, leaving Japan angry and embarrassed because its sovereignty had been violated. The incident ended with Seoul agreeing to Kim's freedom

---

[143] See the "North-South Joint Statement," Columbia Law School, accessed May 16, 2013, http://www.law.columbia.edu.

[144] Lee, *Japan and Korea,* 80–82.

[145] Bruce Cumings, *Korea's Place in the Sun: A Modern History* (New York: W.W. Norton, 2005), 363.

[146] Lee, *Japan and Korea,* 83.

[147] Ibid.

from prosecution for actions taken while in Japan, and Tokyo, in return, agreed to drop the issue. But the incident caused a row between the two countries that would resurface time and again over the next decade.

The second event that strained bilateral ties occurred in August 1974 with the assassination attempt on Park Chung-hee. On 15 August, Mun Se-gwang, a second-generation Korean living in Osaka, Japan, attempted to kill Park during a speech commemorating Korea's liberation from Japan. Park survived the incident unharmed, but his wife, Yuk Young-soo, died from a stray bullet. From Seoul's perspective, Tokyo was to blame because Mun was a permanent Japanese resident who went to the ROK under a forged Japanese passport with false Japanese identity and killed Yuk with a stolen police pistol from Osaka. Tokyo's rejoinder was that Mun was Korean, and the visa that he entered Korea on was issued from the Korean consulate. The situation was defused after U.S. mediation, and Tokyo offered two statements of regret, one written and one oral.[148]

Either the kidnapping or the assassination attempt would have been enough to disrupt ROK-Japanese relations had economic ties not been as strong as they were (Japan became the ROK's largest trading partner in 1966)[149] Despite the heated exchanges over both incidents, Seoul did not elevate Yasukuni as a problem. Timing could explain this outcome: both the kidnapping and the assassination attempt occurred in August, and there were no Yasukuni visits in August either year.

The most compelling explanation why Seoul might have raised Yasukuni during Tanaka's prime ministership would be in response to his April 1974 visit. During a speech he gave to the Diet on 24 January 1974, Tanaka commented that the Japanese occupation of Korea had brought "spiritual benefits" to Koreans.[150] Seoul lodged official objection to Japan, and Tanaka—suddenly on the defensive—denied having made the comment.[151] That Seoul protested Tanaka's comment but ignored his Yasukuni visit two

---

[148] Ibid., 84–85.

[149] Estimate from the Bank of Korea's *Economic Statistics Yearbook, 1961–1983*, cited in Lee, *Japan and Korea*, 88–89.

[150] Quoted in Lee, *Japan and Korea*, 30.

[151] See Seoul Domestic Service in Korea, January 24, 1974, in FBIS *Asia*, January 29, 1974, E2.

months later suggests that Yasukuni did not carry the same significance as the overt reference to the occupation; otherwise Seoul would have objected Yasukuni. The significance of this example is that Korea observers could cite this event as evidence that Seoul manufactured the Yasukuni controversy for political purposes.

### 6. Miki Takeo (1974–1976)

Relations with Seoul improved under Prime Minister Miki, despite continued strain from both the kidnapping and assassination attempt (Tokyo pressed for results from the investigation into the Kim Dae-jung affair while Seoul sought an investigation from Japan on Mun's background). Politically, Tokyo expressed intent to refrain from providing financial support to North Korea at Seoul's request (though Seoul remained skeptical of Tokyo's ties with Pyongyang), the ROK released two Japanese nationals from prison, and both governments collaborated on a response to the communization of Indochina.[152] Economically, trade continued to flourish, increasing 25 percent in 1975 and 65 percent in 1976 from 1973 levels.[153]

In that context, Seoul ignored all three of Miki's Yasukuni visits, including the historic 15 August visit in 1975. The security concerns of communist expansion shared by both Seoul and Tokyo in the wake of the unification of Vietnam, together with presidential candidate Jimmy Carter's campaign pronouncement to remove all ground forces from Korea, likely gave impetus to deal with the larger security concerns ahead of lingering historical animosities.[154]

### 7. Fukuda Takeo (1976–1978)

In 1977, an unresolved territorial dispute over an isolated pair of islets in the Sea of Japan flared, raising bilateral tension amid growing uncertainty in the Northeast Asian security situation rooted in President Carter's plan to withdraw United States ground

---

[152] Haptong in English, January 14, 1975, in FBIS *Asia*, January 14, 1975, E6; Kyodo in English, February 15, 1975, in FBIS *Asia*, February 18, 1975, C1; Seoul Domestic Service in Korean, May 19, 1975, in FBIS *Asia*, May 20, 1975, C4.

[153] Based on figures provided in the Bank of Korea's *Economic Statistics Yearbook, 1961–1983*, cited in Lee, *Japan and Korea*, 88–89.

[154] Lee, *Japan and Korea*, 97.

forces from Korea. Dokdo, or Takeshima in Japan (henceforth referred to as Dokdo), belonged to Korea prior to 1905, but was claimed by Japan after the Russo-Japanese War and subsequent Korean subjugation. After its surrender in World War II, Japan lost claims to the territory it annexed during the Meiji era, including Dokdo. The San Francisco treaty, however, left the Dokdo issue unclear, such that it has been in dispute ever since.

The earliest report of political dispute regarding Dokdo dates back to 1956 under Prime Minister Hatoyama Ichiro (who never visited Yasukuni).[155] The Dokdo dispute erupted in February 1977 when Fukuda made a statement to the Diet that Dokdo belonged to Japan.[156] Tensions increased when Seoul charged that Japan had violated air space over Dokdo later that month.[157] The Dokdo controversy discolored bilateral relations for the remainder of Fukuda's tenure, culminating in calls by the ROK National Assembly to fortify the island (which the ROK government did, building a police facility and observatory station on the island) and Tokyo's decision to suspend 4 million yen in public loans (which were resumed in July 1978).[158] While Dokdo served as an irritant in bilateral ties, given that Fukuda visited Yasukuni in both April and August 1977, one might expect Seoul to protest against Japanese claims over Dokdo by linking it to Yasukuni and the occupation more broadly. But it did not, yet.

### 8. Ohira Masayoshi (1978–1980)

Prime Minister Ohira visited Yasukuni four months after replacing Fukuda in December 1978. Interestingly, rather than object to the visit, ROK Premier and founder of the KCIA, Kim Chong-pil, paid a courtesy call to Ohira on 27 April, one week after Ohira's visit to Yasukuni. Kim expressed Seoul's desire to continue amicable relations with Japan, to which Ohira proclaimed there would be no change in Tokyo's Korea

---

[155] See Seoul in Japanese to Japan, April 23, 1956, in FBIS *Asia*, April 25, 1956, GGG1.

[156] See Haptong in English, February 7, 1977, in FBIS *Asia*, February 8, 1977, E1.

[157] See Haptong in English, February 16, 1977, in FBIS *Asia*, February 16, 1977, E1.

[158] See Haptong in English, November 17, 1977, in FBIS *Asia*, November 17, 1977, E2; Haptong in English, July 26, 1978, in FBIS *Asia*, July 26, 1978, E5.

policy. Yasukuni was curiously absent from the agenda, which suggests that building healthy relations with the new administration took priority over Yasukuni.[159]

Seoul and Tokyo continued to cooperate on security issues under Ohira, evidenced by the joint claims by both governments for Washington to halt its force reduction in the ROK. In 1979, President Carter reversed his 1977 decision to withdraw troops, thus assuaging Seoul's fears of the sudden withdrawal of U.S. forces.[160]

Ties between the two countries remained stable despite the political turmoil following Park Chung-hee's assassination. Former Prime Minister Kishi attended Park's funeral as the special envoy for Japan.[161] Amicable Japan-South Korean ties were disrupted in May 1980, however, following Chun Doo-hwan's military crackdown in Kwangju. The main opposition party in Japan, the Japan Socialist Party, used the incident to pressure the LDP to break political and economic ties with the ROK government. Additionally, Chun's attribution of the Kwangju rebellion to Kim Dae-jung agitated the Japanese public (linking Kwangju back to Kim's kidnapping).[162] The Ohira administration was reluctant to take sides in the affair and, unintentionally, left the inevitable aftermath for his successor to settle.

### 9. Suzuki Zenko (1980–1982)

Prime Minister Suzuki inherited the fallout from Kwangju and the resultant persecution of Kim Dae-jung after Ohira's sudden death. Bilateral ties became quite strained when Suzuki—in response to Kim's conviction and death sentence in July— threatened to suspend financial support to Seoul. Suzuki's comments were reported in Korean media, which ignited anti-Japanese protests in Seoul. The Kim saga carried on into 1981 before intervention by President Ronald Reagan diffused the tension. Meanwhile, Suzuki visited Yasukuni several times, including a mid-August visit. In the midst of the ongoing political upheaval of Chun's consolidation of power and attendant

---

[159] See Haptong in English, April 27, 1979, in FBIS *Asia*, April 27, 1979, E2.

[160] See Haptong in English, June 13, 1979, in FBIS *Asia*, June 13, 1979, E1.

[161] See Haptong in English, November 2, 1979, in FBIS *Asia*, November 2, 1979, E1.

[162] See Kyodo in English, May 27, 1980, in FBIS *Asia*, May 28, 1980, C2.

political suppression, perhaps Yasukuni was not at the forefront of the regime's agenda.[163]

Though the remainder of Suzuki's Yasukuni visits were ignored, there were two significant issues that developed in 1981–1982 that merit special attention. First, Seoul requested considerable loans from Japan to boost its ailing economy. In 1981, the Korean economy was climbing out of the worst slump in twenty years and inflation was rampant. Chun needed an economic stimulus and, in August 1981, sought $6 billion in loans from Japan. The contentious loan negotiations carried on for years, both because of suspicion on the Japanese side that they were tied to the 1965 war reparations and the attendant anti-Korean political climate in Japan that the Kwangju massacre and Kim Dae-jung affair rekindled.[164]

The second issue complicating ROK-Japan ties was Tokyo's revision of Japanese history textbooks in June 1982. Similar to the response in China, a wave of anti-Japanese fervor swept over South Korea, including ROK government denouncement of Japan's actions. The heightened anti-Japanese nationalism continued for months, culminating at the 37th anniversary of Korea's liberation from Japan on 15 August 1982. As part of the occasion, Chun Doo-hwan delivered a commemoration speech highlighting Korean suffering by the Japanese during the colonization period. According to Lee Chong-sik, Chun's speech was notable because it was the first time a ROK president acknowledged South Korea's past weakness as contributing towards its subjugation.[165] Perhaps more important was the impact Chun's words had on Korean society. Lee notes the effects of Chun's speech: "Not even a dictatorial government could contain the strong emotions aroused among the Korean people."[166] On the same day, Suzuki paid tribute at Yasukuni, but the event received no official protests like the textbooks did.

The events of 1981 and 1982 are revealing with regard to Seoul's approach to Yasukuni and the history problem in general. Regarding the ROK's motivation to ignore

---

[163] Lee, *Japan and Korea*, 110–15.

[164] Ibid., 105–22.

[165] Ibid., 147, 217.

[166] Ibid., 147.

Suzuki's Yasukuni visits, logic points to the $6 billion loan request. What incentive did Chun have to make an issue out of Yasukuni and potentially jeopardize badly needed foreign capital over an issue that previously did not merit attention? By shielding the ROK's loan request from historical grievances, Chun was able avoid the historical entanglement that Yasukuni would have brought to the contentious loan negotiations.

On the other hand, the economic argument is weakened by the official protests Seoul lodged with Tokyo over the textbook issue. In the midst of the turbulent loan negotiations, Seoul objected to the textbooks, presumably knowing that such objections might reflect in Tokyo's decision on the amount and terms of the loan, which Seoul had yet to receive.

The textbook controversy is very important in interpreting Seoul's approach to Yasukuni. Chun's 1982 anti-Japanese campaign reached its zenith in August, coinciding with Suzuki's visit to Yasukuni. If Chun aimed to mobilize anti-Japanese nationalism, why did he ignore Suzuki's visit? One might expect Chun to seize upon an easy target— Suzuki's visit—to fuel his rhetorical campaign. Based on the outcome of the 1982 textbook issue, observers might conclude two things: (1) Not all history issues are equal; and (2) economic enhancement initiatives, in and of themselves, cannot outweigh history.

## 10.    Nakasone Yasuhiro (1982–1987)

After Suzuki completed his term (he did not seek reelection), Prime Minister Nakasone ushered in a new era in Japan-ROK relations. Economically, he took decisive action to settle the stalled loan negotiations. Japan agreed to and the ROK accepted a $4 billion loan over seven years, which boosted Seoul's credit rating and stimulated economic recovery.[167] The years following 1982 saw pleasant economic exchanges that were necessary for the implementation of the loans.

Bilateral ties were also improving politically. Nakasone visited Seoul in January 1983, and in 1984 Chun reciprocated and visited Tokyo (a historic first for any ROK

---

[167] Ibid., 131.

president).[168]  During Chun's visit, Nakasone hosted a luncheon on behalf of the visiting president, and commented, "There was a period in this century when Japan brought to bear great sufferings upon your country and its people. I would like to state here that the government and people of Japan feel a deep regret for the error and are determined to firmly warn ourselves for the future."[169]  The joint communiqué produced at the end of the summit detailed various economic, political, and security initiatives both governments would work in concert to achieve, but did not make mention of regret over Nakasone's visits to Yasukuni, or to the history issue more broadly.

Despite significant improvements in bilateral ties, Nakasone visited the shrine several times, including mid-August visits in 1983, 1984, and 1985. None of the visits elicited a response from Seoul. Yasukuni was not mentioned even during Chun's speech commemorating the 40th anniversary of liberation from Japan. The lack of a response to Yasukuni during any of these years suggests that, given China's heated responses to the same events and Chun's active promotion of anti-Japanese rhetoric in 1982, Chun was willing to ignore Yasukuni to seize upon the economic benefits Nakasone was providing.

Chun's tenure as president ended in 1988, making him the last South Korean president to ignore a Japanese prime minister visit to Yasukuni as of this writing. Roh Tae-woo would usher in a new era of Korean politics, and with it a new response pattern to Yasukuni.

## B.  TRANSITIONAL DEMOCRACY SOUTH KOREAN GOVERNMENT RESPONSES TO YASUKUNI

After the transition to democracy in 1988, two Japanese prime ministers visited Yasukuni a total of seven times, and Seoul protested every time. The dramatic reversal of 100 percent non-response to 100 percent protest suggests that the shift to democracy played *a* role in that phenomenon, but could also be attributed to economic development, too.

---

[168] Korean opposition groups criticized Chun's visit to Tokyo on the grounds that it solidified Japanese economic exploitation of the ROK.

[169] Kyodo in English, September 7, 1984, in FBIS *Asia*, September 7, 1984, C5.

## 1. Hashimoto Ryotaro (1996–1998)

The Dokdo dispute flared in early 1996 and Tokyo, despite the usual polemics from both governments, did not recalibrate its approach to Yasukuni. Against the backdrop of renewed Dokdo claims and the return of the LDP to power, Hashimoto's visit on his birthday in July 1996 marked the first time Seoul lodged official protest to the event (contrary to Shibuichi Daiki's argument that Seoul first objected to Yasukuni in 2001). Seoul's response seems to have preempted public opinion in this case, evidenced by its official objection to Hashimoto's visit, which was ahead of Korean media reporting. The ROK government, stating its position on the matter, commented, "In order to build sincere and friendly relations between Japan and Korea it is necessary to respect the feelings of countries which were victims of the attacks by imperialist Japan in the past."[170]  The Korean media echoed the government's response ten days later. In an editorial lambasting Japanese chief cabinet secretary Kajiyama Seiiroku, the *Hanguk Daily* criticized the Japanese rightist trend, stating, "The absurd assertion of Tok-to [Dokdo] belonging to Japan, Prime Minister Hashimoto's visit to Yasukuni Shrine, and Kajiyama's remarks are all of the same vein."[171]  Here, for the first observed time, the linkages of Yasukuni to other lingering historical friction points became clear and should have forewarned Tokyo of a changing political trend in the ROK.

## 2. Koizumi Junichiro (2001–2006)

Prime Ministers Obuchi Keizo (1998–2000) and Mori Yoshiro (200–2001) heeded South Korea's warnings, but Koizumi Junichiro ignored them and visited Yasukuni six times. In response, Seoul objected to all six of Koizumi's visits with steadily increasing levels of rhetoric and action. The ROK government expressed "deep regret" over all six of Koizumi's visits. In 2004, the ROK Foreign Ministry went a step further, strongly urging Koizumi not to visit the shrine again. After Koizumi's 2005 visit, ROK Foreign Minister Ban Ki-moon stated that the single biggest obstacle in ROK-Japan

---

[170] The Digital Chosun Ilbo in English, July 30, 1996, in FBIS *Asia*, July 31, 1996, 38.

[171] Hanguk Ilbo, August 10, 1996, in FBIS *Asia*, August 12, 1996, 48. Kajiyama's comments were in reference to the potential for renewed Korean war reparations demands from Japan following reunification of the Korean peninsula and withdrawal of U.S. forces from Korea.

relations was Koizumi's visits to Yasukuni. Moreover, *Cheong Wa Dae* (the ROK presidential office) threatened to—and did—cancel the December 2005 presidential summit in retaliation.[172] Following Koizumi's 2006 visit, Seoul continued to suspend summits with Tokyo and threatened to freeze the suspension should Koizumi's successor follow in his footsteps.[173]

After Koizumi left office, Tokyo reassessed its approach to relations with its neighbors vis-à-vis Yasukuni. As of this writing, no prime minister has since visited the shrine.

## C.    ANALYSIS OF SEOUL'S RESPONSES

### 1.    Seoul's Responses by the Numbers

Of the 64 visits to Yasukuni, Seoul ignored 57 (89 percent) and responded to seven (11 percent). The breakout of totals by the periods used in this thesis is straightforward: Seoul's authoritarian government ignored every visit while its transitional democracy responded to every visit. Of the seven responses, two were in response to August visits (29 percent), two to January visits, and one each in April, July, and October. By this account, Seoul was as likely to respond to January visits as much as August visits. While it can be said that Seoul is most responsive to August visits, such a

---

[172] Yonhap in English, October 17, 2005, in Open Source Center, accessed May 21, 2013, https://www.opensource.gov/portal/server.pt/gateway/PTARGS_0_0_200_203_121123_43/content/Display/KPP20051017971020#.

[173] Yonhap in English, August 13, 2001, in Open Source Center, accessed May 21, 2013, https://www.opensource.gov/portal/server.pt/gateway/PTARGS_0_0_200_203_121123_43/content/Display/KPP20010813000074; Yonhap in English, April 21, 2002, in Open Source Center, accessed May 21, 2013, https://www.opensource.gov/portal/server.pt/gateway/PTARGS_0_0_200_203_121123_43/content/Display/KPP20020421000039#; Yonhap in English, January 15, 2003, in Open Source Center, accessed May 21, 2013, https://www.opensource.gov/portal/server.pt/gateway/PTARGS_0_0_200_0_0_43/content/Display/PRINCE/KPP20030115000086; Yonhap in English, January 2, 2004, in Open Source Center, accessed May 21, 2013, https://www.opensource.gov/portal/server.pt/gateway/PTARGS_0_0_200_203_121123_43/content/Display/KPP20040102000007#; The Korea Herald in English, August 16, 2006, in Open Source Center, accessed May 21, 2013, https://www.opensource.gov/portal/server.pt/gateway/PTARGS_0_0_200_203_121123_43/content/Display/KPP20060816971108.

random pattern of responses suggests the timing of the visits mattered less than the visits themselves.

## 2.    South Korean Trends and Explanations

A possible explanation for the trend of ignoring Yasukuni up to 1996 lies in its political system. When Park Chung-hee seized power in 1961 he put the ROK on an authoritarian trajectory that lasted until 1988. One of the many hallmarks of an authoritarian state is its ability to steer public opinion, either through fear, repression, coercion, or information dominance. Park's Korea, similar to Mao's China, can be characterized as intolerant of public protests over Japan, or at a minimum dismissive of efforts aimed at harassing Japan (whose economic assistance the ROK relied on, evidenced by Park's determination for diplomatic normalization in 1965). Perhaps Park—whose rise to power was nurtured by the Imperial Japanese Army during the occupation—anticipated the economic benefits that improved bilateral relations with Japan could bring, and made the conscious decision to pursue growth and development rather than dwell on historical animosities. In this context, Park leveraged the power of his office to direct Korea towards industrialization and economic development while minimizing the historical distractions that beset Korea's relations with Japan.

The ROK's authoritarian political system did not stop with Park's assassination in 1979, but rather continued under Chun Doo-hwan. Chun was challenged to consolidate his power early in his tenure and tended to be unsympathetic to public demand for political change, as is evident by his stamping out of any opposition movement such as that in Kwangju in 1980. Considering that Chun wielded significantly less power than his predecessor, one might expect Chun to seize upon anti-Japanese nationalism as a vehicle to help him consolidate power. If this is true, the nearly twenty shrine visits between Prime Ministers Suzuki and Nakasone provided Chun ample opportunity to do so. Yet, even during the highly controversial visit in 1985, Seoul did not register official complaint like Beijing did. Given the lack of any observable response, the political system comes to the fore, again, and presents a case of interests over honor.

By 1985 the ROK was the world's twentieth largest economy—an impressive recovery from the state of economic ruin in 1953—but still far behind Japan. To stimulate continued growth, Chun pursued loans from Japan, the receipt of which having direct implications on Chun's motivations for repressing anti-Japanese nationalism in general (notwithstanding the acute and unanticipated textbook controversy), and specifically with regard to Nakasone's visits to Yasukuni.

After Beijing lambasted Tokyo in the press over Prime Minister Nakasone's 1985 visit to the shrine, it would be 11 years before another Japanese prime minister paid homage at Yasukuni, and it would mark the first time Seoul registered an official objection to a visit to the shrine.

In the context of a democratizing society, political systems appear to have some bearing on anti-Japanese nationalism because the government felt compelled to be responsive to public opinion in a manner different from the previous decades. While many changes happened in Korea socially and politically over the course of the eleven years between Nakasone and Hashimoto's visits to Yasukuni, one significant and undeniable development was a transition from authoritarianism to transitional democracy.

Another interpretation lies in the level of the ROK's economic development in 1996 compared to previous decades. Throughout Park and Chun's tenure, the ROK was highly dependent upon Japanese financing. As that dependency gradually decreased, so too did Seoul's trepidation of challenging Japanese historical provocations. By 1996, after annual growth rates of 9.7 percent since 1965, Seoul had become a high-income economy no longer dependent upon Japan as it once was.[174] Similar to the PRC experience, economic independence from Japan emboldened the ROK to face its past and confront Japan on historical slights. In this context, the transition to democracy made the government more responsive to public opinion, but the ROK's economic prowess sparked the confidence to challenge Japan's policy on prime minister visits to Yasukuni.

---

[174] From 1965 to 1980 the ROK experienced average annual growth in real gross domestic product at 9.9 percent; from 1980–1993, the figure declined slightly to 9.7 percent. See Kosai Yutaka and Takeuchi Fumihide, "Japan's Influence on the East Asian Economies," in *Behind East Asian Growth: The Political and Social Foundations of Prosperity*, ed. Henry Rowen (New York: Routledge, 1998), 299.

## D. CONCLUDING REMARKS

Coming out of the early 1950s, South Korea faced the considerable challenge of rebuilding its war-torn economy, and it needed Japan's help to accomplish the task. In pursuit of this goal, the ROK's authoritarian leaders used their dictatorial power to implement economic and fiscal policies that would improve South Korea's economic and security standing. The post-authoritarian order saw a reversal in Seoul's approach to Japanese provocations, likely because the ROK's economical standing allowed it to challenge Japan without jeopardizing its own national interests.

The non-response pattern observed over Korea's authoritarian period might suggest that the Yasukuni controversy did not resonate with Koreans, but such a conclusion ignores the linkages the symbolism Yasukuni represents to Korean suffering at the hands of early 20th century Japan. Koreans have not forgotten the Japanese occupation or its attendant humiliation and anguish, and to associate governmental disregard of Yasukuni visits with indifference to history would be unwise. The textbook controversy, the Dokdo territorial dispute, and references to the occupation more broadly demonstrate Seoul's recognition of historical grievances and its relentless pursuit to hold Japan accountable for its past actions.

Seoul's response to Yasukuni reveals much about the impact of political systems on anti-Japanese nationalism within a given state. The switch from authoritarianism to democracy brought with it a complete reversal in the government's approach to Yasukuni. Seoul's experience suggests that political systems have some impact on mobilizing nationalism: under the authoritarian banner, Seoul ignored Yasukuni; in a democratic setting, Seoul responded. What happens when Seoul's response is compared to Beijing's? To such an analysis the study now turns.

THIS PAGE INTENTIONALLY LEFT BLANK

# VI. COMPARING POLITICAL SYSTEMS: SIMILARITIES AND DIFFERENCES IN RESPONSE TO YASUKUNI

At this point in the study, both governments' responses to Yasukuni from 1951 to present have been explored and analyzed to explain observed outcomes. The purpose of this chapter is to compare the responses in Beijing and Seoul to each other to assess the impact political systems had on their responses. The argument advanced in this chapter, and the thesis itself, is that the difference in political system had little impact on the responses either government took to Japanese prime minister visits to the Yasukuni Shrine.

Of the 64 shrine visits, the majority (57; 90 percent) occurred during periods of authoritarian governance in both the PRC and ROK. Of these 57 events, similar responses were observed 53 times (93 percent), leaving four responses that differed (seven percent). Moreover, seven visits occurred during the ROK's transition to democracy, of which both governments responded similarly. The preponderance of responses being similar during periods of authoritarian rule, together with 100 percent similar responses from both governments after the ROK transitioned to democracy, supports the argument that the difference in political systems had little impact on the responses either government took to Japanese prime minister visits to the Yasukuni Shrine. The following comparison reviews the similarities and differences in governmental responses and offers additional comparisons and perspectives on the nuanced issues in the Yasukuni controversy.

## A. SIMILARITIES: POLITICAL SYSTEM HAD MINIMAL IMPACT

The comparison criteria used in this study included two primary categories—similar and different—with a secondary category of ignoring a visit or lodging official protest. This section of the chapter focuses on the instances where both governments behaved similarly—meaning both governments either ignored or protested a given visit. The implications of similarities on the study are that similarities suggest that the difference in political system had minimal impact on governmental behavior.

Of the 64 visits to Yasukuni Shrine, similar responses were observed on sixty occasions (93 percent). With over ninety percent of the total number of visits falling into this category, one could reasonably conclude that the difference in political system had little impact on both governments' approach to Yasukuni. A review of the patterns reveals why this is so.

### 1.    Similar-Ignore

Of the sixty similar responses, 53 occurrences (88 percent) resulted in both governments ignoring the visit. Additionally, from 1951 through 1982, both governments consistently ignored prime ministerial visits to Yasukuni, accounting for 45 events. After 1982, eight events revealed the same response, though those were dispersed amongst different responses, and thus inconsistent. Notable in this period is that both governments were authoritarian.

### 2.    Similar-Protest

From Hashimoto's visit in 1996 up to present day, Beijing and Seoul responded to each visit with official protest (seven occurrences, or 12 percent of all similar responses). Notable is that all visits from 1996 forward occurred while the ROK was democratizing (the PRC remained authoritarian). The fact that a transitional democracy behaved similarly to an authoritarian regime is of paramount importance to this study, for it is the strongest evidence suggesting that the difference in political system had little impact on governmental response to Yasukuni. The total number of similar responses (sixty) makes for a strong argument, but more telling is the similarities between two different political systems.

### B.    DIFFERENCES: POLITICAL SYSTEM HAD SIGNIFICANT IMPACT

Differences in governmental response to Yasukuni suggest that the two governments behaved differently to the same stimulus, and therefore the difference in political system may be said to have had a significant impact on governmental response. Evidence reveals that only a small percentage (seven) of the whole registered different responses. As such, the findings were not statistically significant to conclude that political systems impacted governmental behavior. Regarding the categories of differences, while the possibility existed of having cases where one government protested and the other ignored, and vice versa, evidence demonstrated only one pattern of different responses: Beijing protested while Seoul ignored.

Of the 64 visits, Beijing and Seoul differed in their response on four occasions. The four events demonstrated the aforementioned pattern and occurred in August 1982, October 1982, August 1983, and August 1985. Suzuki's August 1982 visit marked the first time a Japanese prime minister visited in an official capacity, and it was the first time Beijing objected to a Japanese prime ministerial visit. Two months later in October, Prime Minister Suzuki visited along with 139 Dietmen, to which Beijing protested. In August 1983, Beijing criticized Nakasone, and again two years later on what would become the most well-known of all Yasukuni visits. Seoul remained quiet on each of these events.[175]

## C.  POLITICIZATION TOPICS: FACT OR FICTION?

Two issues that merit special attention in this chapter—the war criminals' enshrinement and the capacity of prime ministerial visits—are relevant to the discussion and lend themselves well to a comparison. Specifically, comparing Beijing and Seoul's objections to Yasukuni can be revealing in assessing the validity of Tokyo's claim that both governments manufacture the Yasukuni controversy for political reasons. Understanding how and why these two issues impacted governmental response can also help observers explain the timing of each government's decision to respond negatively to Yasukuni.

### 1.  War Criminals

The topic of the 14 Class A war criminals secretly enshrined at Yasukuni in 1978 has been at the forefront of official objections coming out of Beijing and Seoul since 1982. Presuming that both Beijing and Seoul knew about the enshrinement in 1979

---

[175] Seoul responded to other historically significant events over the same time period, such as Japanese history textbook revisions or Tokyo references to the occupation, but not specifically to Yasukuni.

allows certain conclusions to be drawn. Beijing's first official objection to Yasukuni was in August 1982, and a central theme of its criticism focused on the war criminals. With the exception of October 1982, all of Beijing's official protests cite the war criminals as a principle reason why Japanese prime ministers should not visit the shrine. The problem is that there was a delay from the time that the media revealed the enshrinement in 1979 and the first official objection to Yasukuni in 1982. In that three-year period, Japanese prime ministers visited ten times without incident.

Seoul's case is even more egregious. The first time that Seoul mentioned the war criminals was in its 1996 complaint. Between April 1979 and July 1996, Japanese prime ministers visited the shrine 22 times over a period of 17 years without offending Seoul. On the other hand, Seoul mentioned their enshrinement with each official protest.

Regarding the validity of Tokyo's assertion that its neighbors manufactured the war criminals problem for political gain, the years and numbers of shrine visits after the interment and before 1982 for Beijing and 1996 for Seoul supports Tokyo's argument. If the enshrinement of war criminals was the paramount issue in the controversy, then both governments would have objected immediately—either when the story broke or at the first occurrence of a prime ministerial visit after news of the enshrinement (which was April 1979 on both counts). That they did not suggests that both governments manufactured the problem.

Tokyo's argument, however, is weakened when one considers that the first objection from both governments referenced the war criminals. In this context, it is harder to dismiss Beijing and Seoul's claim because to do so would require one to know definitively the reasons why each government objected to Yasukuni when they did. Otherwise, how can one argue that the war criminals were not part of each government's calculus to object?  On the other hand, to say that the war criminals issue was the reason that Beijing responded in 1982 ignores the fact that Beijing followed the Yasukuni controversy with angst since 1969 when the Yasukuni Shrine bill was proposed in Tokyo.

## 2.    Official Capacity of Visits

The second unresolved issue in the Yasukuni controversy is the capacity in which Japanese prime ministers visited the shrine. This issue is a bit more complicated compared to the war criminals' enshrinement, as the latter is a static argument (the war criminals were enshrined 17 October 1978) whereas the former is dynamic in that each prime minister's conduct while visiting determined the extent of the problem.

This thesis credits Prime Minister Suzuki with the first official visit to Yasukuni in August 1982. Once it was made known that Suzuki's visits were official, Beijing consistently objected to them (of which there was only one more before he resigned), which weakens Tokyo's argument. However, Beijing ignored all of Nakasone's visits except for two (1983 and 1985), including four visits after his 1984 pronouncement that all his visits were in an official capacity. In this context, the four visits that Beijing ignored following Nakasone's revelation suggest that Beijing manufactured the problem, thus supporting Tokyo's claim.

Suzuki and Nakasone's pronouncements affected the ROK just as they did the PRC, but in Seoul's case, the government ignored all the "official" visits from both prime ministers. Seoul caught up with the issue during Koizumi's visits, but Seoul's argument that the capacity of the visits stands at the center of the controversy is hindered severely by its dismissal of Suzuki and Nakasone's visits.

## 3.    Summary

The politicization of the war criminals and the capacity of prime ministerial visits is likely to continue as long as Tokyo's national policy on Yasukuni stands at odds with Beijing and Seoul. Of the two politicization issues, it is the author's assertion that the war criminals claim is the more legitimate agitator in the controversy as compared to the capacity issue. The war criminals' enshrinement surfaced with nearly every official objection from both governments. The three years that Beijing ignored visits after learning of the enshrinement weakens its claim, but Beijing's—and Seoul's—consistency afterwards indicates that the issue is not manufactured. Moreover, even if the war criminals claim is being inflated, it is unlikely that Beijing or Seoul will drop the issue, and the farther away the Yasukuni controversy gets from 1982, the less effective Tokyo's rebuttal becomes.

Tokyo stands a greater chance of influencing policy by charging Beijing and Seoul with manufacturing anti-Japanese nationalism on the official capacity issue. For Beijing, the four official visits in between its objections in 1982 and 1985 negate any claim that the official capacity of the visits is what it cannot tolerate. In Seoul's case, too much time passed without objection since 1982 for that argument to be taken seriously.

## D.    CONCLUDING REMARKS

The most compelling evidence supporting the argument of this chapter, and the thesis itself, is that both governments responded similarly to 93 percent of all visits, and that seven of those responses occurred when the ROK was democratizing. That two different political systems behaved the same way in response to a historically significant event reveals much about the similarities and differences in authoritarian regimes and democratic ones. Specifically, it demonstrates an area in which behavior of the two overlaps. With regard to Yasukuni, this finding can aid in assessing the likelihood of future incidents resulting in contention.

It is important to note that the difference in political systems is but one factor contributing towards each government's decision on how to respond to Yasukuni. As mentioned in the previous chapter, Seoul registered its first objection in 1996. By 1996, Seoul became a "high income" economy, evidenced by its ascension into the Organization for Economic Cooperation and Development.[176] The same year saw Seoul lodge its first objection to Yasukuni. Meanwhile, in the PRC, a similar pattern of increased protests to Yasukuni preceded by increased levels of economic development emerged. But the PRC did not democratize (though various democratic elements have been adopted in the PRC in the late 1990s and 2000s). The similarities, therefore, suggest that democracy played a role, but it does not explain the reversal in response to Yasukuni

---

[176] On 12 December 1996, the ROK became the 29th country to join the Organization for Economic Cooperation and Development. See Organization for Economic Cooperation and Development, accessed May 24, 2013, http://www.oecd.org.

in-and-of itself. Economic achievement likely guided both governments into greater assertiveness towards Japan's Yasukuni policy.

Additionally, the impacts of third country intervention (such as the United States or Soviet Union) over time significantly shaped Beijing and Seoul's foreign and security policy, but were outside the scope of this study. Taken together with Korea's example demonstrating an equally compelling link between the economy and foreign policy issues, both warn against monocausal explanations for governmental behavior.

Perhaps more important than the observed trends and explanations is Beijing and Seoul's intent in lodging official protests. The evidence shows that both governments fear revived militarism in Japan. Every official protest by either government contains language dissuading rightist currents in the Japanese government that could lead to a return to militarism. In protesting Yasukuni, Beijing and Seoul seek to influence Japanese foreign and security policy by reminding Japan of its imperialistic past in hopes that Tokyo will stop ignoring the lessons learned from that dark period.

THIS PAGE INTENTIONALLY LEFT BLANK

# VII. CONCLUSION

The purpose of this study was to measure the impact of a difference in political systems on anti-Japanese nationalism. To this end, Japanese prime minister visits to the Yasukuni Shrine proved useful in measuring this impact. Observers might expect that a transitional democracy would respond differently to a given stimulus than an authoritarian regime, but this study found that the difference in political system had little impact on governmental response to Yasukuni. Seoul and Beijing's approach to Yasukuni revealed that more is at play than authoritarianism and democracy, or simply righting historical wrongs. Pursuit of national interests—be they diplomatic, economic, or security—combined with the nuances of political systems influence how each government responds to a historically sensitive issue.

Echoing Stephan Haggard's claim, governmental response to Yasukuni demonstrates the link between economic development and political institutions.[177] The Korean case study suggests that the difference in political system had a significant impact on governmental response vis-à-vis Yasukuni because Seoul's transition to democracy preceded its reversal in response. But what looked like democracy could have been mistaken for economic independence from Japan. Once the ROK was no longer dependent on Japanese economic aid, the government began to challenge Yasukuni where it previously had ignored. The PRC case study reinforces this finding: similar to the ROK, the PRC dramatically reversed its near complete non-response to consistent protest after Nakasone's visit, yet China did not democratize. The conclusion is that the difference in political system had an impact, but the similar trends in response between the PRC and the ROK suggest that governmental response was impacted by political systems and economic development.

---

[177] Stephan Haggard, *Pathways from the Periphery: The Politics of Growth in the Newly Industrializing Countries* (Ithaca: Cornell University Press, 1994), 254.

## A. THE LITERATURE, THE HISTORY, AND THE DATA

### 1. The Literature

The literature on Yasukuni highlights the cultural divide between Japan and its neighbors and stresses the destabilizing effects that Japanese prime minister visits to the shrine have on the region. Scholarship focuses on the Chinese perspective of the debate and misses the opportunity to compare Beijing and Seoul's responses to Yasukuni to assess the impact the difference in political system had on governmental response to Yasukuni. Additionally, the literature on Yasukuni either lacks critical pieces of information (such as the Korean experience) or misrepresents information (Nakasone, for example, is credited with the first official visit when Suzuki did the same thing years earlier), or a combination of both, thus complicating appraisal of the Yasukuni problem.

This study adds original information on the Yasukuni debate by focusing not on the controversy itself, but rather on Beijing and Seoul's responses to it over time. In doing so, the study clarified discrepancies in the information regarding Japanese prime minister visits to the shrine and filled in the gaps previously overlooked by the literature, such as the South Korean side of the debate.

### 2. The History

To understand the depth of the problem one must know the origins of the debate. To this end, the study reviewed the core concepts of the Shinto faith and the unique role Shinto has in the Japanese culture. The study then provided a summary of the Yasukuni Shrine—from its origins in 1869 as a state sponsored war memorial, to its postwar privatization driven by a constitutional separation of religion from state. In 1978, the politics of enshrinement resulted in 14 Class A war criminals being interred at Yasukuni. Since then, neighboring states have politicized the issue, making Yasukuni a place of controversy rather than a place of peace.

### 3. The Data

The study surveyed all Japanese prime minister visits to Yasukuni since 1951. Of the 64 total visits, the preponderance were during the spring and autumn festivals and in commemoration of the end of World War II. The data also revealed key dates and events that add clarity to the Yasukuni controversy: Prime Minister Miki was the first prime minister to commemorate the end of the war on 15 August 1975; Suzuki was the first prime minister to visit Yasukuni in his official capacity on 15 August 1982, and this visit also marked Beijing's first official protest; Nakasone's visit in 1985, while not a first in any sense, resulted in an 11-year hiatus of prime ministerial visits; Hashimoto's 1996 visit marked Seoul's first objection to Yasukuni; and Koizumi's 15 August 2006 visit was the last time a prime minister visited Yasukuni.

## B.    POLITICAL SYSTEMS

The purpose of the thesis was to assess the impact that different political systems had on governmental response to Yasukuni. To this end, the study detailed the typology of political systems and discussed the authoritarian regime in the PRC since its founding in 1949 and the ROK's authoritarian regime since 1948 through its transition to democracy in 1988. In addition to the system, the study focused on the heads of state in both governments over the same period.

The study concluded that political systems and state leadership impacted the approach taken to Yasukuni, but only minimally when compared to another state. That a democratic regime behaved similarly to an authoritarian regime dispels the belief that the two systems would react differently to a historically significant event.

## C.    THE CASE STUDIES

### 1.    The PRC: Changing Leadership, Changing Trends

The PRC case study assessed Beijing's responses to the 64 Japanese prime minister visits to Yasukuni since 1951 and concluded that as state leadership changed, so too did Beijing's response to Yasukuni.[178]  Under Mao, Beijing ignored all Japanese

---

[178] While the undeniable change in leadership coincided with the changed trend in response to Yasukuni, it should be noted that changes in China's economic and security situation over the observed period significantly impacted the internal and external policies the regime pursued. The head of state directed the Party, but observers should compliment any assessment of state leadership with the developments in the strategic environment in which they served.

prime minister visits to Yasukuni. Despite internal Party assessments that China was weak and vulnerable, Mao constructed a "victors" narrative that suppressed anti-Japanese nationalism and drove China's Japan policy, including such measures as refusing war reparations and ignoring prime ministerial visits to Yasukuni.

Deng changed Beijing's approach to Yasukuni. As China's economy began to improve, its Japan policy changed, enabling Beijing to confront Chinese humiliation and suffering at the hands of Japan. Together with the enshrinement of Class A war criminals, Japanese prime minister visits to Yasukuni became too sensitive to ignore. Beijing lodged its first official complaint over Yasukuni in response to Suzuki's 1982 visit. But, similar to his alternating economic advancement and retreat and social liberalization and suppression through the 1980s, Deng's Yasukuni policy vacillated over time. Beijing ignored visits from 1978–1982, protested in 1982, ignored in early 1983 but protested later that year, ignored in 1984, and protested in 1985.

Beijing's leaders after Deng (Jiang Zemin, Hu Jintao) used anti-Japanese nationalism to varying degrees as a mechanism to consolidate power. Beijing responded negatively to all visits from 1996 through 2006. Notable in this period of Chinese political economy is that China had become one of the largest economies in the world.

## 2. The ROK: Changing Government, Changing Trends

Seoul's case provides a useful examination of responses to Yasukuni under both authoritarian and democratic banners. While authoritarian, Seoul ignored all Yasukuni visits. As a transitional democracy, Seoul reversed the trend of ignoring Yasukuni visits in favor of consistent negative responses from 1996 onward.

Prior to Park Chung-hee, Seoul under Rhee Syngman sought to limit engagement with Japan. As a result, the ROK's economic progress stagnated. After Park seized power, engagement with Japan was significantly broadened, seemingly at the expense of settling historical grievances. After Park's assassination, Chun Doo-hwan's pursuit of economic and security improvements revealed a mixed bag of contention and engagement with Japan. While he ignored all Yasukuni visits, Chun responded to the textbook controversy and led a massive anti-Japanese campaign in 1981–1982, all in the midst of considerable loan requests from Japan. Chun then repaired relations with Japan under Nakasone (who at the same time was receiving significant opposition from Beijing on Yasukuni).

In 1988, the ROK's political system changed, and with it came a reversal in Seoul's approach to Yasukuni. From 1996 onward, Seoul objected to Japanese prime minister visits to the shrine. Important to note, however, was that the ROK's economic status had improved significantly from the economic slump that marked the early 1980s. In this context, the change in political system impacted Seoul's Japan policy, but so too did the ROK's improved economic status.

### 3.   Comparisons

The results of the two case studies, when compared to one another, suggest that the difference in political system, while important in other aspects of fomenting or suppressing anti-Japanese nationalism, had little impact on overall governmental response to Yasukuni. Over ninety percent of all Japanese prime minister visits to Yasukuni over the observed period resulted in similar responses. Moreover, 100 percent of all visits after the ROK democratized resulted in similar behavior.

The comparison also revealed similarities in trends between Seoul and Beijing. With the exception of Beijing's vacillation on Yasukuni in the early 1980s, both governments responded negatively from 1996 onward. During that time, one government changed its political system, the other stayed the course; yet, the response was the same (thus weakening the claim that political systems impacted response). Both countries, however, realized significant improvements in global economic standing from the 1990s onward. Thus, the difference in political system had some impact on governmental response, but it alone does not explain the trend.

## D.   POLICY IMPLICATIONS FOR JAPAN

Perhaps equally important to this thesis's findings are the impacts of such on Tokyo's calibration of national policy on prime ministerial visits to Yasukuni. The data suggests—absent predictive analysis—that August visits are more likely (50 percent) to

101

receive negative responses from Japan's neighbors than visits during festivals or other random months.[179] In this context, should Tokyo persist with prime ministerial visits to Yasukuni, it could avoid international outrage by prohibiting prime ministers from visiting in August. Using predictive analysis, the policy implications for Japan are more severe. Beijing and Seoul's protests after every visit since 1996 suggests that the Yasukuni controversy is too entrenched in anti-Japanese emotion that any visit from a Japanese prime minister henceforth is likely to elicit a negative response.[180] In this context, Tokyo would need to prohibit prime minister visits to Yasukuni to avert damaging relations with its neighbors.

Another policy prescription in support of Tokyo's current policy on Yasukuni focuses on economics. Prime ministers may visit Yasukuni and avoid negative responses from Beijing and Seoul if the visit occurs during an economic crisis or downturn in either country. If history repeats itself, economic dependence on Japan would cause Seoul or Beijing to ignore Yasukuni.

If Tokyo ignores the negative responses that Yasukuni generates, it does so at potentially high cost. Korean and Chinese public opinion can and will link Yasukuni to other issues important to Japan, evidenced by the South Korean media reports in 1996 linking Yasukuni to Dokdo and the Chinese protests in 2005 to Japan's bid for permanent membership in the United Nations Security Council. In this context, the protests from the PRC and the ROK jeopardized Japan's attainment of its national goals. On the other hand, by ceding its Yasukuni policy to outside actors, Japanese politicians stand to lose conservative voter support, which can impact the ruling party's maintenance of political power.

---

[179] The data revealed that of all 64 visits to Yasukuni, 43 (67 percent) occurred during the spring and autumn festivals, ten visits (16 percent) occurred in August, and 11 visits (17 percent) occurred outside of either festivals or August. Moreover, of the total 11 events that received official protest, the majority (45 percent) were August visits.

[180] On 21 April 2013, Japanese Prime Minister Abe Shinzo made a ritual offering of a pine tree to the Yasukuni Shrine. The gesture offended Chinese and Korean audiences, causing Beijing and Seoul to lodge official protest. Here, the prime minister did not even visit the shrine, and yet his actions still offended Japan's neighbors. See "Prime Minister Abe's war shrine offering likely to infuriate China," *The Asahi Shimbun*, April 21, 2013, http://ajw.asahi.com.

## E.    CONCLUDING REMARKS

The Chinese proverb, "Past experience, if not forgotten, is a guide for the future" suggests that by ignoring its past, Japan risks a peaceful and harmonious future. China and Korea may never resolve their historical animosity towards Japan, but Japanese provocations like prime minister visits to Yasukuni aggravate the problem and only deepen the historical divide between Japan and its neighbors. Whether China or Korea is authoritarian or democratic matters little in the context of responding to historical grievances when compared to emotion and attitude of those who suffered at the hands of Japanese imperialism. The underlying motivation from both governments is to prevent a resurgence of Japanese militarism. The impetus behind that motivation may wax and wane in relation to each government's goals and objectives at any given time (as this study demonstrates), but—regardless of Beijing or Seoul's economic, security, or political standing—that underlying motivation is strong and will endure. How Japan embraces this reality is for Tokyo to decide, and perhaps it should take stock of what its policy on Yasukuni is in response to.

THIS PAGE INTENTIONALLY LEFT BLANK

| Prime Minister | Term | Visits | Dates Visited | Beijing's Response | Japan-PRC Policy Initiatives | Seoul's Response | Japan-ROK Policy Initiatives | Pattern |
|---|---|---|---|---|---|---|---|---|
| Yoshida Shigeru | 1948-1954 | 5 | October 18, 1951 | No information available | Mao era authoritarianism; Korean War. Popular protests against U.S.-Japan peace treaty | No information available | Korean War. Relationship generally poor under Rhee; Bilateral talks focus on the nationality and status of Koreans in Japan | Similar-Ignore |
| | | | October 17, 1952 | No information available | Mao era authoritarianism, Korean War, 28 Apr 1952: ROC-JP peace treaty. | No information available | Korean War. Relationship generally poor under Rhee; Bilateral talks generally limited to the nationality and status of Koreans in Japan | Similar-Ignore |
| | | | April 23, 1953 | No information available | Mao era authoritarianism, Korean War | No information available | Korean War. Relationship generally poor under Rhee; Bilateral talks generally limited to the nationality and status of Koreans in Japan | Similar-Ignore |
| | | | October 24, 1953 | No information available | Mao era authoritarianism | No information available | Focus on the recent armistice agreement; Relationship generally poor under Rhee; Bilateral talks generally limited to the nationality and status of Koreans in Japan | Similar-Ignore |
| | | | April 24, 1954 | No information available | Mao era authoritarianism; 3 Sep 1954: Taiwan Strait crisis | No information available | Relationship generally poor under Rhee; Bilateral talks generally limited to the nationality and status of Koreans in Japan; Economic focus of protecting ROK infant industries from Japan | Similar-Ignore |
| Hatoyama Ichiro | 1954-1956 | 0 | | | | | | |
| Ishibashi Tanzan | 1956-1957 | 0 | | | | | | |
| Kishi Nobusuke | 1957-1960 | 2 | April 24, 1957 | No information available | Mao era authoritarianism; Kishi's pro-Taiwan stance impaired relations | No information available | Relationship generally poor under Rhee; Bilateral talks generally limited to the nationality and status of Koreans in Japan | Similar-Ignore |
| | | | October 21, 1958 | No information available | Mao era authoritarianism; GLF. Sino-Japanese ties at low point; 23 Aug 1958: Taiwan Strait crisis; 2 May 1958: PRC cuts trade (Nagasaki Flag incident) because of Kishi's support to Taiwan (first prime minister to visit Taipei) | No information available | Relationship generally poor under Rhee; Bilateral talks generally limited to the nationality and status of Koreans in Japan | Similar-Ignore |
| Ikeda Hayato | 1960-1964 | 5 | October 10, 1960 | No information available | Mao era authoritarianism, GLF. Economic enhancement: Friendly trade agreement with Japan | No information available | Relationship generally poor under Rhee; Bilateral talks generally limited to the nationality and status of Koreans in Japan | Similar-Ignore |
| | | | June 18, 1961 | No information available | Mao era authoritarianism, GLF | No information available | ROK domestic political turmoil from Rhee's ousting | Similar-Ignore |
| | | | November 15, 1961 | No information available | Mao era authoritarianism; GLF | No information available | Park Chung-hee rises to power and begins work on normalizing relations with Japan. Strong student opposition to normalization | Similar-Ignore |
| | | | November 4, 1962 | No information available | Mao's retreat from politics; Economic enhancement: LT trade agreement with Japan | No information available | Normalization negotiations | Similar-Ignore |
| | | | September 22, 1963 | No information available | Mao's retreat from politics | No information available | Normalization negotiations | Similar-Ignore |
| Sato Eisaku | 1964-1972 | 11 | April 21, 1965 | No information available | Mao era authoritarianism; PRC hostile to what it termed the "reactionary Sato government"; Japan replaces USSR as PRC's largest trading partner | No information available | Normalization negotiations | Similar-Ignore |
| | | | April 21, 1966 | No information available | Mao era authoritarianism; GPCR. PRC-Japan relations ranked low compared to domestic political upheaval | No information available | 22 June 1965: Relations normalized; Treaty sparks Korean protests that Park crushed | Similar-Ignore |
| | | | April 22, 1967 | No information available | Mao; GPCR; 7 Sep 1967: Sato visits ROC | No information available | Key bilateral policy initiatives not researched due to the significant Korean political suppression from Park's 1965 military crackdown | Similar-Ignore |
| | | | April 23, 1968 | No information available | Mao; GPCR. PRC-JP relations probably ranked low compared to domestic issues. | No information available | Key bilateral policy initiatives not researched due to the significant Korean political suppression from Park's 1965 military crackdown | Similar-Ignore |
| | | | April 22, 1969 | No information regarding Sato's visit. July FBIS report suggests that Beijing objected to the introduction of a shrine law; 1969 is the centennial of Yasukuni | Sato government increased SDF capabilities with additional (104) F4s | No information available | Key bilateral policy initiatives not researched due to the significant Korean political suppression from Park's 1965 military crackdown | Similar-Ignore |

| Prime Minister | Term | Visits | Dates Visited | Beijing's Response | Japan-PRC Policy Initiatives | Seoul's Response | Japan-ROK Policy Initiatives | Pattern |
|---|---|---|---|---|---|---|---|---|
| Sato Eisaku | 1964-1972 | 11 | October 18, 1969 | No information available | Japan Diet introduces the Law of Yasukuni Shrine bill calling for state sponsorship of the shrine; 21 Nov 1969: Sato-Nixon communique suggests Japan's defense role increasing as U.S. presence decreased | No information available | Key bilateral policy initiatives not researched due to the significant Korean political suppression from Park's 1965 military crackdown | Similar-Ignore |
| | | | April 22, 1970 | No information available | Law of Yasukuni Shrine debate | No information available | Key bilateral policy initiatives not researched due to the significant Korean political suppression from Park's 1965 military crackdown | Similar-Ignore |
| | | | October 17, 1970 | No information available | Law of Yasukuni Shrine debate | No information available | Key bilateral policy initiatives not researched due to the significant Korean political suppression from Park's 1965 military crackdown | Similar-Ignore |
| | | | April 22, 1971 | No information available on Sato's visit; A 17 Aug 1971 report suggests that, while not in direct response to a Sato visit, the government bureaucracy was tracking Yasukumi | Reactionary Sato government; Law of Yasukuni Shrine debate; PRC distrustful of Sato, which stalled normalization initiatives started by Sato; 1971: Japan criticism of global "China Fever" | No information available | Key bilateral policy initiatives not researched due to the significant Korean political suppression from Park's 1965 military crackdown | Similar-Ignore |
| | | | October 19, 1971 | No information available | Reactionary Sato government, "stepping up militarist propaganda", Law of Yasukuni Shrine debate; PRC replaces ROC in UN | No information available | Key bilateral policy initiatives not researched due to the significant Korean political suppression from Park's 1965 military crackdown | Similar-Ignore |
| | | | April 22, 1972 | No information available | Diplomatic recognition negotiations; Law of Yasukuni Shrine debate; Normalization initiatives delayed until Sato is succeeded | No information available | Key bilateral policy initiatives not researched due to the significant Korean political suppression from Park's 1965 military crackdown | Similar-Ignore |
| Tanaka Kakuei | 1972-1974 | 5 | July 8, 1972 | No information available | 29 Sep 1972: Diplomatic recognition; Law of Yasukuni Shrine debate | No information available | 4 July 1972: North-South joint statement between Seoul and Pyongyang on reunification | Similar-Ignore |
| | | | April 23, 1973 | No information available | Law of Yasukuni Shrine debate; fall of 1972 at conclusion of normalization treaty in Beijing, Chou Enlai recites the Chinese proverb "The past, if not forgotten, is a guide for the future." | No information available | Key bilateral policy initiatives not researched due to the significant Korean political suppression from Park's 1965 military crackdown | Similar-Ignore |
| | | | October 18, 1973 | No information available | Law of Yasukuni Shrine debate | No information available | 8 Aug 1973: Kim Dae-jung kidnapped from his Tokyo hotel, ignites a row between Seoul and Tokyo | Similar-Ignore |
| | | | April 23, 1974 | No information available on the visit itself, but rather on the Yasukuni Bill | In 1974 China and Japan signed three agreements on trade, aviation and navigation, and the year after, the agreement on fishery; Yasukuni Shrine bill was passed in Diet on 12 Apr & 25 May 1974, however, the bill (submitted every year since 1969) was ultimately defeated due to overwhelming opposition; Sep 1974: Sino-Japanese normalization talks begin. | No information available | 24 Jan 1974: Tanaka comments to Diet that Japanese occupation of Korea brought "spiritual benefits" to Koreans; Feb 1974: Seoul bans Asahi Shimbun from ROK | Similar-Ignore |
| | | | October 19, 1974 | No information available | Agreements on trade, aviation and navigation, and the year after, the agreement on fishery; Normalization negotiations | No information available | 15 Aug 1974: Mun Se-gwang (a Japanese-born Korean) kills Park's wife, Yuk Young-soo, while attempting to assassinate Park | Similar-Ignore |
| Miki Takeo | 1974-1976 | 3 | April 22, 1975 | JP Report suggests contention | Normalization negotiations; 5 Apr 1975: Chiang Kai-shek dies, Miki expresses condolences, Sato attends funeral | JP Report suggests contention | Various political and economical enhancements | Similar-Ignore |
| | | | August 15, 1975 | JP Report suggests contention | Normalization negotiations | JP Report suggests contention | Various political and economical enhancements | Similar-Ignore |
| | | | October 18, 1976 | No information available | Normalization negotiations; 9 Sep 76: Mao dies; Japan implements 1% defense spending cap | No information available | Various political and economical enhancements | Similar-Ignore |
| Fukuda Takeo | 1976-1978 | 4 | April 21, 1977 | No information available | Normalization negotiations | No information available | Various political and economical enhancements | Similar-Ignore |
| | | | April 21, 1978 | No information available | Normalization negotiations; 16 Feb 1978: LT trade; 1978-81: Baoshan project | No information available | Various political and economical enhancements | Similar-Ignore |
| | | | August 15, 1978 | No information available | 12 Aug 1978: Normalized relations | No information available | Various political and economical enhancements | Similar-Ignore |
| | | | October 18, 1978 | No information available | 17 Oct 1978: Class A war criminals interred; 18 Oct 1978: Normalization treaty ratified | No information available | Various political and economical enhancements | Similar-Ignore |

| Prime Minister | Term | Visits | Dates Visited | Beijing's Response | Japan-PRC Policy Initiatives | Seoul's Response | Japan-ROK Policy Initiatives | Pattern |
|---|---|---|---|---|---|---|---|---|
| Ohira Masayoshi | 1978-1980 | 3 | April 21, 1979 | JP Report suggests contention | Feb 1979. Sino-Vietnam War | JP Report suggests contention | Various political and economical enhancements | Similar-Ignore |
| | | | October 18, 1979 | JP Report suggests contention | Hua Guofeng and Ohira exchange visits | JP Report suggests contention | Various political and economical enhancements | Similar-Ignore |
| | | | April 21, 1980 | No information available | Hua Guofeng and Ohira exchange visits | No information available | 18 May 1980: Kwangju Massacre; Tense bilateral diplomacy surrounding the Kim Dae-jung controversy frustrates ROK JP relations. | Similar-Ignore |
| Suzuki Zenko | 1980-1982 | 9 | August 15, 1980 | No information available | | No information available | Hostile bilateral relations; Japanese groups criticize ROK for indicting Kim Dae-jung, Yasukuni was likely ignored due to the much larger Korean political instability at the time | Similar-Ignore |
| | | | October 18, 1980 | No information available | | No information available | Hostile bilateral relations. Tension over Kim Dae-jung verdict | Similar-Ignore |
| | | | November 21, 1980 | No information available | December 1980: First Sino-Japanese Ministerial conference in Beijing | No information available | Jan 1981: Chun regime initiated a massive anti-Japanese campaign; 20 Nov 1980: Korean protesting of Japanese interference in the Kim Dae-jung trial | Similar-Ignore |
| | | | April 21, 1981 | No information available | Jan 1981 PRC unilaterally cancels Baoshan project | No information available | In accordance with the Reagan-Suzuki talks, Japanese economic aid to ROK as part of the U.S. anti-Soviet strategy; Aug 1981: Seoul requested $6 billion from Tokyo | Similar-Ignore |
| | | | August 15, 1981 | No information available | Japan provides 300 billion yen Baoshan loan | No information available | Turbulent loan negotiations | Similar-Ignore |
| | | | October 17, 1981 | No information available | | No information available | Turbulent loan negotiations | Similar-Ignore |
| | | | April 21, 1982 | No information available | December 1981: Second Sino-Japanese Ministerial conference in Tokyo | No information available | Turbulent loan negotiations; June 1982: ROK lowers request to $4 billion; Textbook controversy frustrates bilateral relations, consuming time of both governments | Similar-Ignore |
| | | | August 15, 1982 1st official Prime Minster Visit; 1st official objection (PRC) | Minimal objection as reported in Renmin Ribao linking Suzuki's visit to lessons not learned from World War II; Minimal observable response (Xinhua simply reported that the visit occurred); Though reporting demonstrates that Suzuki attended in an official capacity, yet no int'l outrage as seen in 1985 | 26 June 1982: Japanese textbook controversy; 1 Sep 1982: 12th CCP Congress, Deng needed diversion | No information available | Turbulent loan negotiations; 26 June 1982: Textbook controversy flared, despite the ongoing loan negotiations | PRC Protest-ROK Ignore |
| | | | October 18, 1982 | Xinhua criticizes the visit of 139 Dietmen to Yasukuni, but not about Suzuki's visit, though a causal link can be inferred | | No information available | Turbulent loan negotiations; textbook controversy frustrates bilateral ties | PRC Protest-ROK Ignore |
| Nakasone Yasuhiro | 1982-1987 | 10 | April 21, 1983 | No information available | Nakasone's transition to office improved Sino-Japanese relations | No information available | Bilateral ties begin to improve: 30 Nov 1982: Nakasone orders MOFA to settle loan negotiations; 30 Dec 1982: ROK accepts $4 loan over a seven-year period; 11 Jan 1983, Nakasone historic state visit to Seoul (to which Chun reciprocated in 1984) | Similar-Ignore |
| | | | August 15, 1983 | Renmin Ribao criticized Nakasone, printing an article on 21 Aug, "The Past, If Not Forgotten, is a Guide for the Future." | | No information available | A "new era of partnership": Implementation of Japanese loans | PRC Protest-ROK Ignore |
| | | | October 18, 1983 | No information available | Beijing requests $5 billion loan from Tokyo | No information available | A "new era of partnership": Implementation of Japanese loans | Similar-Ignore |
| | | | January 5, 1984 | Searched FBIS, no PRC response available; "Protesters" cited in Kyodo, but no way to know who those protesters were, and this happened in Tokyo, so they were likely Japanese | Loan negotiations | Searched FBIS, no Seoul response available; "Protesters" cited in Kyodo, but no way to know who those protesters were, and this happened in Tokyo, so they were likely Japanese | A "new era of partnership": Implementation of Japanese loans | Similar-Ignore |
| | | | April 21, 1984 | No information available | Loan negotiations | No information available | A "new era of partnership": Implementation of Japanese loans | Similar-Ignore |
| | | | August 15, 1984 | No information available | Loan negotiations; 10 Aug 1984. Nakasone announces visit will be official, just as his previous visits were. | No information available | Anti-Japanese student protests in Seoul demanding Chun cancel trip to JP (Chun visited 6-8 Sep 1984); Chun was criticized in Korea for beliefs that his trip was furthering Japanese economic exploitation of Korea; 8 Sep 1984. Chun-Nakasone Joint Communique | Similar-Ignore |

| Prime Minister | Term | Visits | Dates Visited | Beijing's Response | Japan-PRC Policy Initiatives | Seoul's Response | Japan-ROK Policy Initiatives | Pattern |
|---|---|---|---|---|---|---|---|---|
| Nakasone Yasuhiro | 1982-1987 | 10 | October 18, 1984 | No information available | Loan negotiations | No information available | Chun Doo-hwan visited Japan; Chun requested additional loans | Similar-Ignore |
| | | | January 21, 1985 | No information available | Loan negotiations | No information available | | Similar-Ignore |
| | | | April 22, 1985 | No information available | Loan negotiations | No information available | 7 May 1985: 23rd Korea-Japan Cooperation Council in Seoul; No mention from either government regarding Yasukuni or history | Similar-Ignore |
| | | | August 15, 1985 | 14 Aug 1985: MOFA said a visit would hurt the world's feelings; Deng criticized Nakasone; comments made at Grand Assembly of 40th anniversary of war; 18 Sep 85: mass students demonstrations in Beijing and Qianghua; 3 Oct 1985: 1000-student protest in Xian | | No information available | Political rhetoric directed at Japan is conspicuously absent in Chun's 40th Anniversary of liberation speech; 8 Sep 1986: ROK foreign minister cancelled historic foreign ministers meeting | PRC Protest-ROK Ignore |
| Takeshita Noboru | 1987-1989 | 0 | | | | | | |
| Uno Sosuke | 1989-1989 | 0 | | | | | | |
| Kaifu Toshiki | 1989-1991 | 0 | | | | | | |
| Miyazawa Kiichi | 1991-1993 | 0 | | | | | | |
| Hosokawa Morihiro | 1993-1994 | 0 | | | | | | |
| Hata Tsutomu | 1994-1994 | 0 | | | | | | |
| Murayama Tomiichi | 1994-1996 | 0 | | | | | | |
| Hashimoto Ryutaro | 1996-1998 | 1 | July 29, 1996 | Beijing protested against Prime Minister Hashimoto's visit to Yasukuni Shrine and Senkaku island issue | Bilateral relations at a low point: The LDP returned to power after a 3-yr hiatus; Beijing conducted a highly politicized nuclear test in 1995 and fired missiles at ROC in March 1996 | ROK media criticized Hashimoto's visit; Official government statement denouncing Hashimoto's action | | Similar-Protest |
| Obuchi Keizo | 1998-2000 | 0 | | | | | | |
| Mori Yoshiro | 2000-2001 | 0 | | | | | | |
| Koizumi Junichiro | 2001-2006 | 6 | August 13, 2001 | PRC MOFA called Koizumi's announcement to visit, "difficult to understand" and insisted it contradicted Japan's desire to "develop friendly relations"; Negotiations resulted in an agreement for a 13 Aug visit vice 15 Aug; Post-visit Renmin Ribao voiced strong condemnation of the visit | Textbook revision; Lee Tenghui visited Japan | Seoul expressed "strong regret"; Kim Dae-jung personally criticized Koizumi's visit | | Similar-Protest |
| | | | April 21, 2002 | China postponed both Minister of State for Defense Nakatani Gen's visit to China and the first visit of Chinese naval vessels to Japan (planned for 14 May 2002); PRC MOFA criticized Koizumi's visit | | Seoul expressed "deep regret" | Co-host 2002 FIFA World Cup | Similar-Protest |
| | | | January 14, 2003 | Renmin Ribao highly critical of visit and of Koizumi's attempt to mitigate damage by changing date of visit to Jan. | | Seoul expressed "deep regret" | | Similar-Protest |
| | | | January 1, 2004 | MOFA criticized Koizumi in the lead up to the 2004 visit, and after | | Seoul expressed "deep regret" | | Similar-Protest |
| | | | October 17, 2005 | Wen Jiabo refused to meet with Koizumi; MOFA criticized visit. | | ROK Foreign Minister Ban Ki-moon expressed "deep regret and disappointment" over visit; Cheong wa Dae cancelled December presidential summit | Roh Moo-hyun refused to meet with Koizumi | Similar-Protest |
| | | | August 15, 2006 | PRC MOFA, Renmin Ribao, and Hu criticized Koizumi | | Seoul expressed "deep regret"; Cheong Ha Dae threatened to cease state visits with Tokyo if Abe visited Yasukuni | | Similar-Protest |

| Prime Minister | Term | Visits | Dates Visited | Beijing's Response | Japan-PRC Policy Initiatives | Seoul's Response | Japan-ROK Policy Initiatives | Pattern |
|---|---|---|---|---|---|---|---|---|
| Abe Shinzo | 2006-2007 | 0 | | | | | | |
| Fukuda Yasuo | 2007-2008 | 0 | | | | | | |
| Aso Taro | 2008-2009 | 0 | | | | | | |
| Hatoyama Yukio | 2009-2010 | 0 | | | | | | |
| Kan Naoto | 2010-2011 | 0 | | | | | | |
| Noda Yoshihiko | 2011-2012 | 0 | | | | | | |
| Abe Shinzo | 2012- | 0 | | | 21 Apr 2013: Abe made ritual offering of a pine tree to Yasukuni, to which Beijing objected | | 21 Apr 2013: Abe made ritual offering of a pine tree to Yasukuni; ROK Foreign Minister Yun Byung-se cancels trip to Tokyo | |

| | Total Visits: | 64 | | Spring/Autumn Festival Visits: 43 (67%) | August Visits: 10 (16%) | Non-Festival, Non-Aug Visits: 11 (17%) |
|---|---|---|---|---|---|---|

| Similar responses: 60/64 or 93% | Different responses: 4/64 or 7% | Similar-Ignore: 53 | Similar-Protest: 7 |
|---|---|---|---|

| PRC Protest-ROK Ignore: 4 |
|---|

THIS PAGE INTENTIONALLY LEFT BLANK

# LIST OF REFERENCES

"Agreement Between Japan and the Republic of Korea Concerning the Settlement of Problems in regard to Property and Claims and Economic Co- Operation." *International Legal Materials* 5, no. 1 (1966): 111–117.

Akaha, Tsuneo. "Japanese Security Policy in Post-Cold War Asia." In *The Major Powers of Northeast Asia: Seeking Peace and Security*, edited by Tae-hwan Kwak and Edward Olsen. Boulder: Lynne Reinner, 1996.

———. "The Nationalist Discourse in Contemporary Japan: The Role of China and Korea in the Last Decade." In *Pacific Focus* 23, no. 2 (2008): 156–88.

"Bilateral Political Relations." China Internet Information Center. Accessed May 2, 2013. http://www.china.org.cn.

Blasko, Dennis. *The Chinese Army Today*. New York: Routledge, 2012.

Borton, Hugh. *Japan's Modern Century*. New York: Ronald Press, 1955.

Breen, John. "Introduction: A Yasukuni Genealogy." In *Yasukuni, the War Dead, and the Struggle for Japan's Past*, edited by John Breen. New York: Columbia University Press, 2008.

———. "Yasukuni and the Loss of Historical Memory." In *Yasukuni, the War Dead, and the Struggle for Japan's Past*, edited by John Breen. New York: Columbia University Press, 2008.

Calder, Kent. "China and Japan's Simmering Rivalry." In *Foreign Affairs* 85, no. 2 (2006): 129–39.

Cha, Victor. "Japan-Korea Relations: On Track and Off Course (Again)." Accessed November 20, 2012. http://csis.org/files/media/csis/pubs/0104qjapan_korea.pdf.

"Charter of the International Military Tribunal for the Far East." *The Avalon Project at the Yale Law School*. Accessed March 29, 2013. http://avalon.law.yale.edu.

"The Common Program of the Chinese People's Political Consultative Conference," (1949). Accessed April 3, 2013. http://e-chaupak.net/database/chicon/1949/1949e.pdf.

"The Constitution of the People's Republic of China." (2004). Accessed April 3, 2013. http://www.npc.gov.cn/englishnpc/Constitution/node_2825.htm.

Cotton, James. "From Authoritarianism to Democracy in South Korea." *Political Studies* 37, no. 2 (1989): 244–259.

Cummings, Bruce. *Korea's Place in the Sun: A Modern History*. New York: Norton, 2005.

Dahl, Robert. *Dilemmas of Pluralist Democracy: Autonomy vs. Control.* New Haven: Yale University Press, 1982.

Deans, Phil. "Diminishing Returns? Prime Minister Koizumi's Visits to the Yasukuni Shrine in the Context of East Asian Nationalisms." *East Asia* 24 (2007): 269–94.

Fackler, Martin. "Japanese Politician's Visit to Shrine Raises Worries." *The New York Times*. Accessed November 20, 2012. http://www.nytimes.com/2012/10/18/world/asia/japan-opposition-leader-shinzo-abe-visits-war-shrine-a-possible-message-to-neighbors.html.

Gang, Qian, and David Bandurski. "China's Emerging Public Sphere: The Impact of Media Commercialization, Professionalism, and the Internet in an Era of Transition." In *Changing Media, Changing China*, edited by Susan Shirk. Oxford: Oxford University Press, 2011.

Gries Peter. *China's New Nationalism: Pride, Politics, and Diplomacy*. Los Angeles: University of California Press, 2004.

———. "China's 'New Thinking' on Japan." *The China Quarterly*. Accessed November 20, 2012. http://www.ou.edu/uschina/gries/articles/texts/GriesCQ.pdf.

Griffith, Ed. "The Three Phases of China's Response to Koizumi and the Yasukuni Shrine Issue: Structuration in Sino-Japanese Relations." *European Research Center on Contemporary Taiwan Online Paper Series* (2012).

Ha, Yong-chool. "South Korea in 2001: Frustration and Continuing Uncertainty." *Asian Survey* 42, no. 1 (2002): 56–66.

Haggard, Stephan. *Pathways from the Periphery: The Politics of Growth in the Newly Industrializing Countries.* Ithaca: Cornell University Press, 1994.

Harootunian, Harry. "Memory, Mourning, and National Morality: Yasukuni Shrine and the Reunion of State and Religion in Postwar Japan." In *Nation and Religion: Perspectives on Europe and Asia*, edited by Peter Van Der Veer and Hartmut Lehmann. Princeton: Princeton University Press, 1999.

He, Yinan. "History, Chinese Nationalism and the Emerging Sino-Japanese Conflict." *The Journal of Contemporary China* 16, no. 50 (2007): 1–24.

Hirokawa, Takashi, and Sangim Han. "Japan Ministers Visit War Shrine as Ties With S. Korea Fray." *Bloomberg Businessweek*. Accessed November 30, 2012. http://www.businessweek.com/news/2012–08–14/japan-minister-visits-war-shrine-fraying-ties-with-south-korea.

Hsiao, Gene. "The Sino-Japanese Rapprochement: A Relationship of Ambivalence." In *Sino-American Détente and Its Policy Implications*, edited by Gene Hsiao. New York: Praeger, 1974.

Hwang, Jihwan. "Rethinking the East Asian Balance of Power." *World Affairs* 166, no. 2 (2003): 95–108.

Iriye, Akira. "Chinese-Japanese Relations, 1945–90." *The China Quarterly*, no. 124 (1990): 624–38.

Itoh Mayumi. *Pioneers of Sino-Japanese Relations.* New York: Palgrave Macmillan, 2012.

Johnson, Chalmers. "South Korean Democratization: The Role of Economic Development." *The Pacific Review* 2, no. 1 (1989): 1–10.

———. "The Patterns of Japanese Relations with China, 1952–1982." *Pacific Affairs* 59, no. 3 (1986): 402–28.

Kosai, Yutaka, and Takeuchi Fumihide. "Japan's Influence on the East Asian Economies." In *Behind East Asian Growth: The Political and Social Foundations of Prosperity*, edited by Henry Rowen, 297–318. New York: Routledge, 1998.

Lee, Chong-sik. *Japan and Korea: The Political Dimension.* Stanford: Hoover Institution Press, 1985.

Lee, Won-deog. "A Normal State Without Remorse: The Textbook Controversy and Korea-Japan Relations." *East Asian Review* 13, no. 3 (2001): 21–40.

Levitsky, Steven, and Luncan Way. "The Rise of Competitive Authoritarianism." In *Readings in Comparative Politics: Political Challenges and Changing Agendas*, edited by Mark Kesselman. Boston: Wadsworth CENGAGE Learning, 2010.

Lieberthal, Kenneth. *Governing China: From Revolution through Reform.* New York: W.W. Norton, 2004.

Lind, Jennifer. "The Perils of Apology: What Japan Shouldn't Learn From Germany." *Foreign Affairs* 88, no. 3 (2009): 132–46.

Matthews, Eugene. "Japan's New Nationalism." In *Foreign Affairs* 82, no. 6 (2003): 74–90.

McClain, James. *Japan: A Modern History.* New York: Norton, 2002.

Miller, Alice, and Richard Wich. *Becoming Asia: Change and Continuity in Asian International Relations Since World War II.* Stanford: Stanford University Press, 2011.

Moon, Chung-in, and Seung-won Suh. "Identity Politics, Nationalism, and the Future of Northeast Asian Order." In *The United States and Northeast Asia*, edited by John Ikenberry and Chung-in Moon. Lanham: Rowman and Littlefield, 2008.

Morley, James. *Japan and Korea: America's Allies in the Pacific*. New York: Columbia University, 1965.

Onishi, Norimitsu. "Japan and South Korea Brace for a Tense Meeting." *The New York Times*, November 20, 2012. http://travel.nytimes.com/2005/06/20/international/asia/20seoul.html?_r=1&page wanted=print&.

Park, Cheol-hee. "Cooperation Coupled with Conflicts: Korea-Japan Relations in the Post-Cold War Era." *Asia-Pacific Review* 15, no. 2 (2008): 13–35.

Perry, Elizabeth. "Permanent Rebellion? Continuities and Discontinuities in Chinese Protest." In *Popular Protest in China*, edited by Kevin O'Brien. Cambridge: Harvard University Press, 2008.

Qiang, Xiao. "The Rise of Online Public Opinion and Its Political Impact." In *Changing Media, Changing China*, edited by Susan Shirk. Oxford: Oxford University Press, 2011.

Ono, Sokyo. *Shinto: The Kami Way*. Rutland: Tuttle Publishing, 1962.

Open Source Center. Accessed May 24, 2013. https://www.opensource.gov.

Organization for Economic Cooperation and Development. Accessed May 24, 2013. http://www.oecd.org.

"Prime Minister Abe's war shrine offering likely to infuriate China." *The Asahi Shimbun*, April 21, 2013. http://ajw.asahi.com.

Przystup, James. "Japan-China Relations: Cross Currents." Institute for National and Strategic Studies. The National Defense University. Accessed May 6, 2013. http://csis.org/files/media/csis/pubs/0304qjapan_china.pdf.

Reilly, James. *Strong Society, Smart State*. New York: Columbia University Press, 2012.

Rose, Caroline. "Breaking the Deadlock: Japan's informal diplomacy with the People's Republic of China, 1958–9." In *Japanese Diplomacy in the 1950s: From Isolation to Integration*, edited by Iokibe Makoto, et al. New York: Routledge, 2008.

———. "Stalemate: The Yasukuni Shrine Problem in Sino-Japanese Relations." In *Yasukuni, the War Dead, and the Struggle for Japan's Past*, edited by John Breen. New York: Columbia University Press, 2008.

Ryang, Sonia. "Koreans in Japan." *Amerasia Journal* 29, no. 3 (2003): 31–35.

Ryu, Yong-wook. "The Yasukuni Controversy: Divergent Perspectives from the Japanese Political Elite." *Asian Survey* 47, no. 5 (2007): 705–26.

Samuels, Richard. *Securing Japan*. Ithaca: Cornell University Press, 2008.

Santayana, George. *The Life of Reason*. Amherst: Prometheus Books, 1998.

Sasajima, Masahiko. "Japan's Domestic Politics and China Policymaking." In *An Alliance for Engagement: Building Cooperation in Security Relations with China*, edited by Benjamin Self and Jeffrey Thompson. Washington, DC: The Henry L. Stimson Center, 2002.

Scott, Geoffrey. "Spoliation, Cultural Property, and Japan." *Law Journal Library*. Accessed May 15, 2013. http://home.heinonline.org.

Seaton, Phillip. "Pledge Fulfilled: Prime Minister Koizumi, Yasukuni and the Japanese Media." In *Yasukuni, the War Dead, and the Struggle for Japan's Past*, edited by John Breen. New York: Columbia University Press, 2008.

Shibuichi, Daiki. "The Yasukuni Shrine Dispute and the Politics of Identity in Japan: Why All the Fuss?" In *Asian Survey* 45, no. 2 (2005): 197–215.

"The Shinto Directive." *Contemporary Religions in Japan* 1, no. 2 (1960): 85–89.

Shirk, Susan. "Changing Media, Changing China." In *Changing Media, Changing China*, edited by Susan Shirk. Oxford: Oxford University Press, 2011.

———. "Changing Media, Changing Foreign Policy." In *Changing Media, Changing China*, edited by Susan Shirk. Oxford: Oxford University Press, 2011.

———. *China: Fragile Superpower*. New York: Oxford University Press, 2008.

Shuli, Hu. "The Rise of Business Media in China." In *Changing Media, Changing China*, edited by Susan Shirk. Oxford: Oxford University Press, 2011.

Soeya, Yoshihide. *Japan's Economic Diplomacy with China, 1945–1978*. Oxford: Clarendon Press, 1998.

Stockmann, Daniela. "What Kind of Information Does the Public Demand? Getting the News During the 2005 Anti-Japanese Protests." In *Changing Media, Changing China*, edited by Susan Shirk. Oxford: Oxford University Press, 2011.

Sturgeon, William. *Japan's Yasukuni Shrine: Place of Peace or Place of Conflict?* Boca Raton: Dissertation.com, 2006.

"Syngman Rhee." *The Cold War Files.* The Wilson Center. Accessed April 8, 2013. http://legacy.wilsoncenter.org/coldwarfiles/index-33794.html.

Tamamoto, Massaru. "A Land Without Patriots: The Yasukuni Controversy and Japanese Nationalism." *World Policy Journal* 18, no. 3 (2001): 33–40.

Takenaka, Akiko. "Enshrinement Politics: War Dead and War Criminals at Yasukuni Shrine." *The Asia-Pacific Journal: Japan Focus.* Accessed May 15, 2013. http://www.japanfocus.org.

Tanaka, Hitoshi. "Japanese Foreign Policy Under Prime Minister Yasuo Fukuda." *East Asia Insights* 2, no. 6 (2007): 1–4.

Thornton, Patricia. "Manufacturing Dissent in Transnational China." In *Popular Protest in China*, edited by Kevin O'Brien. Cambridge: Harvard University Press, 2008.

Tiewes, Frederick. "The Establishment and Consolidation of the New Regime, 1949–1957." In *The Politics of China*, edited by Roderick MacFarquhar. Cambridge: Cambridge University Press, 2011.

"Treaty on Basic Relations between Japan and the Republic of Korea." *Database of Japanese Politics and International Relations.* Institute of Oriental Culture, University of Tokyo. Accessed April 8, 2013. http://www.ioc.u-tokyo.ac.jp/~worldjpn/documents/texts/docs/19650622.T1E.html.

U.S. Foreign Broadcast Information Service. *Daily Report: Asia and Pacific.* Washington, DC: GPO.

Wang, Fei-Ling. "Chinese Security Policy in Northeast Asia." In *The Major Powers of Northeast Asia: Seeking Peace and Security*, edited by Tae-hwan Kwak and Edward Olsen. Boulder: Lynne Reinner, 1996.

Whiting, Allen. *China Eyes Japan.* Berkeley: University of California Press, 1989.

Yasukuni Shrine Webpage. Accessed November 20, 2012. http://www.yasukuni.or.jp/english/index.html?mode=skip.

Zhixin, Wang. "China, Japan and the Spell of Yasukuni." In *Yasukuni, the War Dead, and the Struggle for Japan's Past*, edited by John Breen. New York: Columbia University Press, 2008.